BUCKNELL REVIEW

# Rhetoric, Literature, and Interpretation

STATEMENT OF POLICY

BUCKNELL REVIEW is a scholarly interdisciplinary journal. Each issue is devoted to a major theme or movement in the humanities or sciences, or to two or three closely related topics. The editors invite heterodox, orthodox, and speculative ideas and welcome manuscripts from any enterprising scholar in the humanities and sciences.

Contributors should send manuscripts with a self-addressed stamped envelope to the Editor, Bucknell University, Lewisburg, Pennsylvania 17837.

BUCKNELL REVIEW

# Rhetoric, Literature, and Interpretation

Edited by
HARRY R. GARVIN

Special Associate Editor This Issue
Steven Mailloux

LEWISBURG
BUCKNELL UNIVERSITY PRESS
LONDON AND TORONTO: ASSOCIATED UNIVERSITY PRESSES

Associated University Presses, Inc.
440 Forsgate Drive
Cranbury, NJ 08512


Associated University Presses Ltd
25 Sicilian Avenue
London WC1A, 2QH, England


Associated University Presses
2133 Royal Windsor Drive
Unit 1
Mississauga, Ontario, Canada L5J 1K5

**Library of Congress Cataloging in Publication Data**
Main entry under title:

Rhetoric, literature, and interpretation.

  (Bucknell review; v. 28, no. 2)
  1. Criticism—Addresses, essays, lectures.
2. English literature—History and criticism—
Addresses, essays, lectures.   I. Garvin, Harry R.,
1917–    .   II. Series.
AP2.B887 vol. 28, no. 2 [PN85] [809] 051s 83-2553
ISBN 0-8387-5057-5

**(Volume XXVIII, Number 2)**

Printed in the United States of America

# Contents

Recent Issues of *Bucknell Review*

# Notes on Contributors

MARYLIN B. ARTHUR: Teaches at Wesleyan University. Writes and lectures on women in antiquity, archaic Greek poetry, and psychoanalysis and literary criticism. Currently completing "The Dream of a World without Women: Vision and Design in the Works of Hesiod."

MICHAEL HANCHER: Teaches at the University of Minnesota, where he is co-editor of *Centrum*. Has published many essays and reviews on literary theory, speech-act theory, Robert Browning, and other topics.

BURTON HATLEN: Teaches at the University of Maine at Orono. Publications and current research: Shakespeare, Milton, Gothic fiction, and modern poetry.

JAMES M. HEATH: Chairman of the Department of Classics at Bucknell University. Professional interests in Greek and Roman history, literature, and philology. Associate Editor of *Bucknell Review* since 1976.

STEVEN MAILLOUX: Teaches critical theory and American literature at the University of Miami. Has published *Interpretive Conventions: The Reader in the Study of American Fiction.* Currently working on the institutional history of American literary studies.

ALGIS MICKUNAS: Teaches at Ohio University. Main interests: Continental thought, comparative civilizations, cross-cultural communication, and cultural symbols of consciousness. Recent article: "Perception in Husserl and Merleau-Ponty." Forthcoming: translations of J. Gebser, *Ursprung und Gegenwart* (Origin and Presence) and E. Stroeker, *Philosophische Untersuchungen zum Raum* (Philosophical Investigations of Space); "Dimensions of Language" in his collection of essays *Comparative Studies of Cultures* (in German).

DANIEL O'HARA: Teaches at Temple University. Forthcoming: *Tragic Knowledge: Yeats's Autobiography and Hermeneutics.* Has written essays on irony in twentieth-century literature and criticism.

DANIEL STEMPEL: Teaches at the University of Hawaii at Manoa. Articles on literature and philosophy in *PMLA, Journal of the History of Ideas, Mosaic,* and others. Now working on a book-length study of changes in discourse and epistemology in eighteenth- and nineteenth-century literature.

ROBERT WESS: Teaches at Oregon State University. Essays on *Tom Jones* and Perry Anderson's *Arguments within English Marxism.* Forthcoming: reviews of Paul Hirst's *On Law and Ideology* and Fredric Jameson's *The Political Unconscious.* Principal interests: Kenneth Burke, Fredric Jameson, literature and society.

DAVID WILLBERN: Teaches at SUNY at Buffalo. Member, Center for the Psychological Study of the Arts. Has published on Kyd, Shakespeare, D. H. Lawrence, Freud. Current projects: Shakespeare and book on Elizabethan and Jacobean revenge drama (a psychoanalytic study).

# Introduction

Since antiquity, critics of literature have been searching to understand what they do when they practice their craft, art, or game. They find criticism torn in inescapable dichotomies: theory and practice, understanding and evaluation, description and analysis, instruction and entertainment, rhetoric and interpretation. Dichotomies like these suggest roles and functions for the critic, but they leave the nature of the critic in doubt. In what way can critics exist in their own right when challenged by all the ancillary functions that enter into criticism: those of the teacher, mystic, philologist, historian, philosopher, moralist, not to mention the most powerful challengers, the rhetorician and the literary artist? The critic's role must often be defined in relation to one or more of such roles as these, in opposition or cooperation or in some more complex relationship. This issue of *Bucknell Review* singles out one pair of oppositions that define the role of the critic, interpretation and rhetoric, and presents three groups of essays to illustrate the problems critics face when they adopt one side of this dichotomy as a starting premise, the ingenious strategies they may employ to exploit and justify that initial premise, and the consequences of attempting a resolution of the dichotomy. Each set of essays contains contributions that explore a particular critical theory or practice or both; all seek to illustrate particular approaches and to delineate their limiting features.

The first set of essays investigates criticisms that start out as interpretations of literature, attempts to derive or create hitherto unrealized meanings in literary works. In his essay on Milton, Mary Shelley, and patriarchy, Burton Hatlen attempts to recover a revolutionary content in both *Paradise Lost* and *Frankenstein* by reading the works in conjunction. Traditionalist critics, he argues, have seen in the works traces of the mythos of a dominating patriarch creator. Hatlen, however, maintains that the signs in *Frankenstein* point in a different direction, toward a mythos of creativity with a nonmale creator. Such a mythic content, he adds, better fits the revolutionary context of Milton and Mary Shelley and illuminates her creative process and critical reading of Milton.

In an essay that deals with literary and critical theory rather than practice, Algis Mickunas discusses recent developments in hermeneutics. After tracing briefly the history of that term's use before Hans-Georg Gadamer, he assesses Gadamer's achievement. First, Mickunas distinguishes Gadamer's "hermeneutics" from the "apophantics" of Martin Heidegger. Heidegger attempts to attain understanding by extracting an expression from the context within which it functions; hermeneutics, for Gadamer, attempts to understand the context. Such an understanding of context depends upon linguistic understanding—thereby gaining insight into the presuppositions imbedded in language—and upon understanding the historical tradition that has produced that language. "Human understanding is immersed in a historically effective consciousness."

The problem of the nature of the knowledge that gives such an understanding exercises the successors of Gadamer, who denied the validity or effectiveness of science without linguistic understanding; for he and his successors asserted that science cannot attain knowledge about itself. Erich Heintel explores more closely the dominating role that the technological model of the explanatory sciences adopts and argues for a more humanistic hermeneutic that, unlike the scientific, allows hermeneutics to understand itself. Karl-Otto Apel searches for a model of a domain of mediation between the scientific and humanistic approaches and suggests the encounter of Western technology and pretechnical societies where differing hermeneutical traditions come into conflict. Otto Poeggeler goes a step further by integrating a technological hermeneutical model within the humanistic through the use of his "mantic phenomenology." Finally, however, Poeggeler is still left with the need for a mediator and reverts to the image of Hermes, the founding conception and eponym of hermeneutics, the god that translates divine edicts into human language.

Marylin Arthur sets out to explore one kind of psychoanalytic interpretation of literature, the application of the Narcissus motif, the self-reflexive project of male identity to recover itself as presence. Allied with the doubled presence of Narcissus lies its correlate, the doubled absence of Echo, the other. Such pairing of oppositions poses difficulties for understanding the female writer who eludes such facile polarization. H. D., who was both a poet and a patient of Freud, offers a challenge to the validity of the approach through Narcissus. Her feminist outlook and awareness of psychoanalytic theory render problematic the simplistic application of "Freudian" interpretation. Arthur examines H. D.'s poem "Red Roses for Bronze" as a challenge to produce an alternative to a standard Freudian reading, and achieves a feminist interpretation that restores meaning by unmasking the illusions the poem introduces.

These essays have presented or challenged recognized interpretative approaches that offer the possibilities of both complementing and excluding other approaches. David Willbern's approach, which he terms *hypocriticism*, brings into play, when appropriate, the whole range of activities critics use: close reading techniques, personal memories, verbal associations, and much more, including the standard approaches of the "schools" of psychology and so on. A "hypocritical" reader becomes a participant in a poem's dialogue and a partner or "rival" of its author, in that word's etymological sense. Willbern displays his hypocritical interpretative method on Robert Duncan's "My Mother Would Be a Falconress," bringing that poem to life through the experiences and emotions of his own life.

The two essays of the second set treat criticism from a rhetorical standpoint. One might argue—in a broad way—that when critics "interpret" a text they are helping the reader against the author of that text, real or implied, to posit a meaning over which the author has little or no control. A rhetorical criticism, on the other hand, sees the critic helping an author against the reader, real or implied, investigating and supplementing the techniques the author uses to manipulate the reader, creating for the author a work whose meaning the reader cannot easily tamper with. Naturally, these two approaches are not exclusive. The interpreter can lay aside for a moment a reader's mask and adopt that of the author, and a rhetorician can abandon an author's role. The typical rhetorical strategy is based on the discovery or creation by the critic of a structure that the author devises or which constrains him; the existence of this structure permits the investigation of the effect of a text on a reader in predictable if not always desirable or ethical ways.

To illustrate an extreme version of rhetorical criticism,

Daniel Stempel's essay examines one kind of underpinning of the New Formalism, the critical approach rooted in the use of structural linguistics or its analogues, which adopts paradigms from the physical, biological, and human sciences. Structuralists can assume the linking of the languages of literature and economics. Two contemporary critics, Marc Shell and Kurt Heintzelman, have argued that the discourse of literature and economics intersects in common elementary constituents: metaphorical exchanges. This assumption permits them a formal procedure for criticizing a wide range of texts. Stempel, too, argues for an "economic" reading of texts, but his method transcends a simplistic, ahistorical formalism by positing the need to search for imaginative constitutive paradigms. These paradigms fulfill rhetoric's need for some kind of formalism. Stempel attempts to focus on these paradigms in isolation from the other feature of rhetoric, concern with language that calls attention to itself, by devoting the second part of his essay to an examination of Wordsworth's "Michael: A Pastoral Poem," a work written in ordinary language stripped of metaphor. Stempel's concluding section shows the limitations of applying Shell and Heintzelman's economic readings to Marxist and other contemporary texts for which the method might seem well suited. The rhetorical formalism to which they aspire cannot deal with the immediacies of the language and paradigms of such texts.

Robert Wess considers a somewhat similar kind of question, as he discusses Louis Althusser's revisions in the understanding of Marx's thought. He focuses on the concept of totality which Althusser opposes to that of economism, "a misreading of Marx inspired by Hegelian dialectic." The simplistic formalism of base and superstructure that economism postulates leads to a reductionistic method of textual analysis through the ideologies that are assumed to derive mechanistically from the economic base. Wess focuses on the term *ideology* as the bridge in this argument. He traces the development of the term in the thought of Althusser, his sources, and his commentators, especially Antonio Gramsci and Fredric Jameson. Wess sees the core of the problem of ideology as its nature: is it a kind of physical entity, as traditional Marxism postulates, and thus the subject of science, or something else, a proper subject for humanistic study? Althusser finds both extreme positions untenable and hence seeks to locate ideology in the problematic of signification. Here, ideology becomes a "symbolic action with persuasive power in concrete social and economic situations." Ideology, in other words, is a form of rhetoric and needs to be treated accordingly.

The theory—and practice—of interpretation can be derived from disciplines ancillary or alien to literary criticism; interpretations may be sweeping and general or individual and tailored to the demands of a particular work. An interpretation balanced between the sweeping and the particular, the literary and the nonliterary, is hard to attain. The interpreter is concerned always with the range, power, and applicability of interpretation. On the other hand, the rhetorical critic tends to be limited by the power of structures and rules of language and warned away from sweeping, open-ended readings of literary texts. It is not surprising, therefore, that, to attain depth and sensitiveness, critics resort to a combination of often contradictory methods of reading. The two final essays in this issue illustrate how rhetorical and interpretative approaches may interact, in harmony or conflict.

Daniel O'Hara is concerned with the tendency of deconstructionist critics to identify "onto-theological traditions" at work in the texts they study and to master the discourse of these texts by this identification. Any idea of a self—author or reader—becomes a fiction in such readings; the critic's reading is needed to make a text clear and whole. But, as Paul de Man argued, the critic's reading, too, becomes a text to deconstruct in its own right. To avoid infinite regression, deconstructionists resort to "irony": "preliminary sketches for a parodic interpretation of the critic" that privilege the critic's position.

To get around this regression, O'Hara uses *Women in Love* to demonstrate a position that combines interpretative and rhetorical elements. He shows how Lawrence in that work anticipates the position Michel Foucault developed in his analysis of sexuality as a complex round of pleasure-knowledge-power. Lawrence invents the discourse of human sexuality and also seeks to evade that discourse by making sex sacred and unnameable. Exploring the consequences for criticism of this irony in Lawrence's text, O'Hara argues that it is not an exclusively linguistic phenomenon. Lawrence, he argues, leaves himself a true "nothing," a randomness that possesses the same kind of power as death.

The final paper takes up a topic that appears to belong to the area of rhetoric, but it develops an interpretative approach by elucidating for a reader the effect of a text. Michael Hancher analyzes the madness in *Through the Looking-Glass* by examining the pragmatics of the conversations in that work, starting from the approaches of J. L. Austin and John Searle but presenting also the approaches of other scholars who have applied pragmatics and speech-act theory to literary texts. Hancher is able to show how Carroll's characters manipulate Alice and how Alice learns to ignore or circumvent the unfamiliar devices of the characters she encounters. Hancher's discussion is essentially rhetorical, in its insistence on study of the linguistic text through formal structures. But this study helps to convey to the reader a sense of the real-life situations imbedded in the text and hence a sense of the author's motives and strategies. Ultimately, Hancher argues, this insight begins to make clear the meaning of that elusive literary term *tone*.

The editors hope that the essays of this issue of *Bucknell Review* contribute some light to the ongoing struggles of critics to elucidate literature and to analyze their elucidations.

James M. Heath
Associate Editor

# Rhetoric, Literature, and Interpretation

# Interpretation and Literature

# Milton, Mary Shelley, and Patriarchy

## Burton Hatlen

### University of Maine

BOTH John Milton and Mary Shelley were revolutionary writers: Milton in his advocacy of individual liberty in an epoch of aristocratic and theocratic tyranny, and Mary Shelley in her exploration of the corrosive effects that inequalities of power and status exercise on personal relations. But bourgeois literary criticism has attempted in various ways to obscure the revolutionary implications of the works of both these writers. The author of *Paradise Lost* has been transformed by critics like Douglas Bush and C. S. Lewis into an apostle of Christian orthodoxy—"enchanted," says Lewis, by "the Hierarchical principle."[1] And recently there has been a concerted effort to remold the author of *Frankenstein* into a nervous conservative who projected onto her Monster her fears of the unwashed masses.[2] To recover the revolutionary content of the works of Milton and Mary Shelley, it is useful, I believe, to read *Frankenstein* and *Paradise Lost* in conjunction. For *Frankenstein* is at least in part a commentary on and amplification of *Paradise Lost*, designed to uncover certain egalitarian and libertarian motifs that are at work in Milton's poem, but which are there partly suppressed by an overlay of religious orthodoxy. That there is a direct connection between *Frankenstein* and *Paradise Lost* has not gone unnoted by the critics, but the principal discussions of the relationship between these texts have been distorted by the already mentioned conservative bias of most recent criticism. For example, Leslie Tannenbaum, seeing *Paradise Lost* as purely and simply a defense of divine authority, argues that Mary Shelley's allusions to Milton primarily serve to establish a contrast be-

19

tween the legitimate power and authority of God and Victor
Frankenstein's illegitimate claims to a similar power and authority.[3] No less than the conservative Tannenbaum, the cultural feminists Sandra Gilbert and Susan Gubar also obscure
the revolutionary content of both the texts here under discussion. Gilbert and Gubar see Milton as the archetypal misogyn-
ist. *Paradise Lost,* they argue, sets out to show that women are
responsible for all the ills of humankind. And the "divagations"
of Mary Shelley's parody, they contend, "merely return to and
re-inforce the fearful reality of the original. For by parodying
*Paradise Lost* in what may have begun as a secret, barely conscious attempt to subvert Milton, Shelley ended up telling, too,
the central story of *Paradise Lost,* the tale of 'what misery the
inabstinence of Eve / Shall bring on men!'"[4] Unlike both Tannenbaum on the one side and Gilbert and Gubar on the other, I
believe (and, perhaps more to the point, the Romantics also
believed) that *Paradise Lost* conceals some unexpectedly revolutionary implications. And I further believe that the purpose of
Mary Shelley's parody of *Paradise Lost* is, not to reveal the in-
adequacy of would-be human imitators of God, nor to reassert
Milton's presumed view of woman as the source of all evil, nor
even to "subvert Milton"—but rather to explode what I shall
here call the patriarchal mythos of creation. According to the
patriarchal mythos, the act of creation is the exclusive preroga-
tive of the male of the species, and it entails rights of ownership
both over the "means" of creation (that is, the female) and over
the end result of this act. This patriarchal mythos is central to
*Paradise Lost;* therefore Mary Shelley develops her critique of
patriarchy primarily through a series of allusions to Milton's
poem. But like most of the Romantics Mary Shelley seems to
assume that Milton was secretly on the side of the rebel against
patriarchy. Therefore her goal is less to "destroy Milton" than
to liberate the "true" Milton from this false mythos. Her secondary aim, I propose, is to point toward an alternative mythos
of cooperation and equality, in the belief that only such a
mythos can resolve the sterile struggle between creator and
creature. It is the struggle between these two mythoi, the
mythos of patriarchy and the mythos of equality, as that struggle unfolds within the dialogue between Mary Shelley and John
Milton, that I shall attempt to trace out in the pages that follow,
with the ultimate goal of recovering the revolutionary energies
that Mary Shelley in her time discovered in *Paradise Lost,* and

the revolutionary hopes to which she herself gave expression in
*Frankenstein.*[5]

I

Mary Shelley was the child of two of the principal revolutionary thinkers of her epoch, and the wife of still another such
thinker. William Godwin contributed to the emergent revolutionary thought of the nineteenth century a careful analysis of
the destructive psychological effects that the master/servant,
superior/inferior, ruler/ruled relationship has on both parties
to such transactions. *Caleb Williams* dramatizes the master/slave
dialectic more powerfully than any other book of the period,
except *Frankenstein* itself, and in the *Enquiry Concerning Political
Justice* Godwin develops a thorough critique of government,
which he sees as a system designed to preserve inequalities of
power and privilege.[6] Although he had little awareness of the
ways in which government serves or subverts economic interests, Godwin rigorously pursued the theory that any form of
inequality limits and distorts human potential by condemning
"inferiors" to lives of passive dependence and jealous rage, and
by encouraging laziness and self-indulgence in "superiors."
Mary Wollstonecraft extended this analysis to male/female relations, arguing that political and economic inequality between
men and women prevented women from developing into rational, responsible human beings. The supposed inadequacies
of women are, Wollstonecraft argued, a consequence of rather
than a justification for the power of men over women.[7] Godwin
and Wollstonecraft were drawn together by their common belief that all forms of inequality between human beings are destructive—a belief which both of them articulated vigorously,
and upon which they acted courageously (sometimes, at least).
The revolutionary commitments of Godwin and Wollstonecraft
put them at the center of the English group (a group that
included Thomas Paine and William Blake) who supported the
French Revolution and dedicated themselves to the principles
of that revolution: liberty, equality, fraternity. Almost two cen-
turies after the French Revolution, the words that served as its
rallying cry may seem threadbare. And some Marxists may take
pleasure in dismissing the French Revolution and its principles
as "bourgeois." Yet the demand for liberty and equality is still a
powerfully revolutionary act, as the civil rights and women's

movements have recently demonstrated. And any revolution worthy of the name must still incorporate these ideals, even though twentieth-century revolutionary movements usually demand types of equality (economic, social) that go far beyond the demands of the early proponents of political equality. The Godwin/Wollstonecraft critique of inequality thus continues to be "radical," and it remains an essential component of our revolutionary heritage. All the English Romantics owed a debt to the radical egalitarianism of Godwin and his circle. In particular, Percy Shelley, who became Godwin's son-in-law, sought in many of his poems to give expression to certain revolutionary theories that he had developed in part through a careful study of Godwin's *Enquiry*. The writings of Godwin and Wollstonecraft and the daily conversation of Byron, Percy Shelley, and other radicals established the intellectual environment within which Mary Shelley wrote *Frankenstein*. Mary Shelley's diary indicates that during the time she was writing *Frankenstein* she read and reread the works of both her parents, and that Percy Shelley read aloud to her all of Milton's works—a reading presumably interspersed with discussions of the implications of these poems. And when the book was finished, she dedicated it to her notorious father. Clearly, then, if we wish to understand the metamorphosis that Milton's treatment of the patriarchal mythos undergoes in the crucible of Mary Shelley's imagination, we cannot ignore the effects upon her of the libertarian and egalitarian ideals that pervaded her environment.

If we wish to understand Mary Shelley's response to Milton, we must also recognize that for the thinkers who most influenced her the importance of Milton's work lay not in his apparent defense of traditional conceptions of hierarchy and obedience but rather in what the Romantics saw as his half-suppressed but still powerful inclination to subject to a ruthless critique all forms of inequality and arbitrary power. To the Romantics, Milton was a great hero in the ongoing human struggle for liberty and equality. The Romantics, Joseph Wittreich notes, saw Milton as "a 'revolutionary artist,' which means that he works with, not within, poetical traditions and that he criticizes the very systems—political and theological— that he postulates in his poetry and prose."[8] Blake's summation of this Romantic conception of Milton was seminal: "The reason Milton wrote in fetters when he wrote of Angels and God, and at liberty when of Devils and Hell, is that he was a true poet

and of the Devil's party without knowing it."[9] The emphasis
here on the disparity between Milton's conscious intent and the
actual effects of his verse, between his apparent celebration of
authority (God's over Satan and man, Adam's over Eve) and his
latent sympathy for the rebel who rejects all claims to authority,
is typical of Romantic commentary on Milton. In the *Enquiry*
Godwin echoes Blake's description of Satan as the archetype of
the rebel against arbitrary authority: "Why did [Satan] rebel
against his maker? It was, as he himself informs us, because he
saw no sufficient reason for that extreme inequality of rank and
power which the creator assumed."[10] Even Mary Wollstonecraft, while noting that many passages in *Paradise Lost* imply a
derogatory view of women, saw a conflict within Milton between an overt belief in male superiority and a latent desire for
male/female equality: "It would be difficult," she says, "to render two passages which I now mean to contrast, consistent."
And she then juxtaposes Eve's statement to Adam ("God is thy
law, thou mine") with Adam's own request that God create for
him a mate who will be his equal ("Among unequals what society / can sort, what harmony or true delight?").[11] Finally, and
perhaps most significantly, Percy Shelley consistently saw *Paradise Lost* as a profoundly subversive critique of arbitrary authority:

> Milton's Devil as a moral being is as far superior to his God, as One
> who perseveres in some purpose which he has conceived to be
> excellent in spite of adversity and torture, is to One who in the cold
> security of undoubted triumph inflicts the most horrible revenge
> upon his enemy, but with the alleged design of exasperating him to
> deserve new torments.[12]

And in *Prometheus Unbound,* Shelley set out, it would seem, to
rewrite *Paradise Lost:*

> The only imaginary being resembling in any degree Prometheus, is
> Satan, and Prometheus is, in my judgment, a more poetical charac-
> ter than Satan, because, in addition to courage, and majesty, and
> firm and patient opposition to omnipotent force, he is susceptible
> of being described as exempt from the taints of ambition, envy,
> revenge, and a desire for personal aggrandisement, which, in the
> Hero of *Paradise Lost,* interfere with the interest.[13]

This statement by Shelley invites us to see *Prometheus Unbound*
as a "purified" *Paradise Lost* in which the false crust of "orthodoxy" that overlays Milton's poem is stripped away to liber-

ate the revolutionary myth hidden within, and in this effort to uncover the presumed latent but "true" content of Milton's poem, Percy Shelley's poetic drama establishes itself as part of one of the major projects of Romanticism—the ongoing effort to rescue Milton from Christian orthodoxy.

William Godwin, Mary Wollstonecraft, and Percy Shelley all influenced the developing intellect and imagination of Mary Shelley, and *Frankenstein* represents, I here wish to propose, both a powerful synthesis of the responses to Milton summarized above and an important step forward in the dialogue (a dialogue centered upon the themes of authority and equality) between the Romantics and Milton. Mary Shelley shared with her husband an empathy with the rebel against arbitrary authority. But for her, as U. C. Knoepflmacher has shown, authority embodied itself with particular intensity in the figure of her own father, William Godwin.[14] Mary Shelley found herself in the role of the Other standing over against the Father, legitimate authority, in two ways: first as child, and second as female. For Mary, then, the relationship between the master who claims authority and the rebel who denies that claim became intertwined with the relationships between creator and creature and between man and woman. In *Paradise Lost* Mary Shelley found all of these linked analogies at work. *Paradise Lost,* before it is a poem about sin and the Fall, is a poem about creation, and thus inevitably a poem about the mutual rights and responsibilities of the creator and the creature. *Paradise Lost* is also, inevitably but in some ways surprisingly, about the relationship of male and female—a relationship that assumes an archetypal form in the story of Adam and Eve. Milton inherited certain ideas and images on all of these matters from the Bible specifically (which gave him, for example, the story that Eve was created out of Adam's rib) and more broadly from the Judeo-Christian heritage (his image of Satan, for example, derives more from folklore and the Church Fathers than from the Bible). In pulling together this complex of material *Paradise Lost* offered Mary Shelley, as it offered many other English writers, an invaluable summation of the Judeo-Christian mythos of creation—or as I have here described it, the mythos of patriarchy. But Milton also, as his prose writings on politics and on marriage demonstrate, had some novel, occasionally revolutionary, ideas of his own on the relationship of rulers to ruled and of men to women. In *Frankenstein* Mary Shelley responds to all these dimensions of *Paradise Lost:* the "traditional" and the "revolutionary," the cosmological and the psychological, the political and the personal. Like Percy Shelley in *Prometheus Unbound,* Mary Shelley has set out to rewrite *Paradise Lost*—not as tragedy but rather as nightmare, perhaps even as farce. Because *Frankenstein* draws together all the principal motifs of Milton's poem, it seems to me a more subtle response to *Paradise Lost* than is *Prometheus Unbound.* Mary Shelley recognizes the degree to which inequalities of power distort not only our cosmogonic myths and our political institutions but also (and Percy was blind to this point) our family structures and sexual relations. Thus Mary pushes beyond Percy's critique of arbitrary power to develop a critique of the total cultural and psychological system that in our society sustains relations of inequality both in and outside the family. And as the patriarchal mythos dissolves in the corrosives of Mary Shelley's parody, the possibility of an alternative mythos also moves into the foreground. In this respect *Frankenstein* not only "liberates" the "hidden" content of *Paradise Lost* but also, I here want to argue, moves beyond not only Milton's poem but also any text by Mary Shelley's own contemporaries in the attempt to discover a genuine alternative to patriarchy.

## II

The central act of *Paradise Lost* is the act of Creation, in all senses of that term. In book 7, the poem retells and elaborates the story of the creation of the universe, as told in Genesis. But in *Paradise Lost* the divine act from which issues the natural world is preceded and followed by many other acts of creation. Long before the creation of the material world, God himself had generated his son:

> This day I have begot whom I declare
> My only Son, and on this holy hill
> Him have anointed, whom ye now behold
> At my right hand. Your head I him appoint;
> And by myself have sworn to him shall bow
> All knees in heav'n, and shall confess him Lord.
> [*PL* 5.603–8][15]

At some indefinite period earlier still, God presumably also created heaven and all the angels—although they are unable to remember this moment when they came into being. But Satan too possesses at least a negative power to generate new life. In parody of God's creation of the Son, Satan gives birth to Sin, an event that Sin herself describes as follows to her father:

> All on a sudden miserable pain
> Surprised thee; dim thine eyes, and dizzy swum
> In darkness, while thy head flames thick and fast
> Threw forth, till on the left side op'ning wide,
> Likest to thee in shape and count'nance bright,
> Then shining heav'nly fair, a goddess armed
> Out of thy head I sprung.
>
> [*PL* 2.752–59]

And, more broadly, Satan's rebellion against God seems to "create" Hell:

> Anon out of the earth a fabric huge
> Rose like an exhalation, with the sound
> Of dulcet symphonies and voices sweet. . . .
>
> [*PL* 1.710–12]

The human characters in the poem also display creative powers, which seem to increase as the poem proceeds. Adam asks God for a mate, and God grants this request by allowing Adam to "give birth" to Eve, just as God gave birth to the Son and Satan to Sin. Adam describes this event to Raphael as follows:

> Mine eyes [God] closed, but open left the cell
> Of fancy, my internal sight, by which
> Abstract as in a trance methought I saw,
> Though sleeping, where I lay, and saw the Shape
> Still glorious before whom awake I stood;
> Who stooping opened my left side, and took
> From thence a rib, with cordial spirits warm,
> And life-blood streaming fresh; wide was the wound,
> But suddenly with flesh filled up and healed.
> The rib he formed and fashioned with his hands;
> Under his forming hands a creature grew,
> Man-like, but different sex, so lowly fair. . . .
>
> [*PL* 8.460–71]

Later, Adam and Eve, by violating God's command, create for themselves a new identity: they become sinners. And later still, by first forgiving one another and then asking forgiveness of God, they create for themselves still other identities, as repentant sinners. All these changes are mediated through language.

Adam and Eve become steadily more loquacious as the poem
proceeds, and the most memorable speeches of both characters
come after the Fall; in effect, they recreate themselves through
language. Finally, but not incidentally, both God's creation of
the universe and the struggle of Adam and Eve to create themselves through language find a counterpart in the poet's own
struggle to perform a verbal act that will, if not create the
world, at least justify it and himself. "O Spirit," the poet prays,

> that dost prefer
> Before all temples th' upright heart and pure,
> Instruct me, for thou know'st; thou from the first
> Wast present, and with mighty wings outspread
> Dove-like sat'st brooding on the vast abyss
> And mad'st it pregnant: what in me is dark
> Illumine, what is low raise and support;
> That to the highth of this great argument
> I may assert Eternal Providence,
> And justify the ways of God to men.
>
> [*PL* 1.17–26]

As a poem about creation, *Paradise Lost* thus also becomes a
poem about its own creation—a process in which the poet becomes both (consciously) an imitator and (unconsciously) a rival
to God.

From my (and also, I think, from Mary Shelley's) point of
view, the significance of Milton's description of the process of
creation arises from his unusually detailed exposition of what I
have called the patriarchal mythos of creation, and from his
own apparent uneasiness about this mythos. Milton did not
invent this mythos. Rather, he inherited it from his sources
(both the Bible and Greek philosophy), and he absorbed it from
his environment. To the seventeenth century, the patriarchal
conception of creation was, quite simply, true, and Milton
seems to have accepted it as such. I call this conception of
creation "patriarchal" because it assumes that the generative
power is exclusively male. The female is at best a "vessel" that
temporarily contains and nurtures the new life generated by
the male. This conception of the process of creation derives
directly from the Bible: the famous list of "begats" in the first
chapter of Matthew suggests that each male in the line of David
generated his own son, with at best incidental assistance from
an occasional woman. On the theological level, the doctrine that
a (male) God single-handedly generated the universe reflects

and reinforces the belief that the generative power is uniquely male. And at least in the rigidly masculinist gospel of John, God also seems to generate his own son in (apparently) a single act of the will, and in turn the son with his own hands shapes Adam out of the dust. In demonic parody of these processes, Satan generates Sin out of his own head, and on earth Adam himself gives birth to Eve, by an operation not unlike Caesarian section. Until the last books of the poem, then, the power to give birth is a power almost exclusively exercised by males. (The one exception is Sin, who engages in incestuous intercourse with her father and as a consequence gives birth to Death.) It should also be noted that in all these instances of male birth, the creature is in some degree "lesser" than his creator. The son "is" God, but he is also contained within his father, who is thus "larger" than he. The Son creates Adam, a clearly inferior being, and Adam, after giving birth to Eve, learns from Raphael that he should treat her as an inferior:

> For what admir'st thou, what transports thee so,
> An outside? Fair no doubt, and worthy well
> Thy cherishing, thy honoring, and thy love,
> Not thy subjection. Weigh with her thyself;
> Then value. Ofttimes nothing profits more
> Than self-esteem, grounded on just and right
> Well managed; of that skill the more thou know'st,
> The more she will acknowledge thee her head,
> And to realities yield all her shows. . . .
>
> [PL 8.567–75]

There seems to be a general principle here: the "male mother" in some fashion "owns" the creature to which he gives birth. Nor can the "Son" ever grow up, to become the "Father" in his own right. The Son is, eternally, the Son. So too Eve is presumably intended by God to remain forever an obedient appendage of Adam. Again Sin, the mother of Death, is the exception that seems to prove the rule. Born of woman, Death is *not* an obedient extension of his mother. Rather, he sullenly threatens both his mother and his father, who control him only by promising that someday he will be permitted to satiate freely his appetites. At this point the pattern seems clear. The creator, if he is male and if he gives birth without the intercession of woman, "owns" the creature. It is an extension of him, and, theoretically at least, it finds its fulfillment in obeying him. The patriarchal cosmos, it seems, is a perfectly hierarchical world, descending by stages from God, the "author" of all creation. And each creature in this hierarchy, recognizing that it owes its existence to a creator who occupies a higher level in the hierarchy, responds (or in theory should respond) with gratitude and obedience.

Insofar as *Paradise Lost* postulates as the original order of things a perfectly hierarchical world, the poem may seem to lend credence to the currently widespread theory that Milton was a proponent of order, tradition, authority—and masculine superiority. However, it is difficult to reconcile this image of Milton with his political career as a defender of the Puritan rebellion against royal authority. In *The Tenure of Kings and Magistrates* Milton insists that any claim to authority must be subject to the test of reason. In *Areopagitica* he vigorously defends the right of all people to learn and grow through experience, and implicit in this defense of free speech is a conception of the autonomous individual as rightfully free to shape an identity through responsible moral choices. In the divorce tracts, finally, he predicates the possibility, indeed the necessity, of intellectual equality between men and women. That Milton does not argue for legal equality as well (a man, he proposes, should have the right to divorce a woman who is not his intellectual equal, but he does not propose that this same right be extended to women) shows that he was subject to the limitations of his epoch. But the furor that these tracts provoked offers support for the Romantic view of Milton as the most advanced social thinker of his epoch. In *Paradise Lost* itself there are also some signs that Milton felt a certain ambivalence toward the patriarchal mythos. Milton's insistence that we look at God's authority from Satan's viewpoint is one sign of this ambivalence. But even more significant is Milton's treatment of the central figures of his poem, Adam and Eve. Satan's rebellion against God's authority ends in sterility and despair, but the disobedience of Adam and Eve proves to be a creative, a "fruitful" act. Satan promises Eve that eating the forbidden fruit will make men "like God," and one of the central ironies of the poem is that this promise proves perfectly correct. By sinning, Adam and Eve become self-creating beings who shape their destinies by their own choices rather than automata capable only of obedience. The disobedience of Adam and Eve thus subverts irrevocably the neatly hierarchical universe predicated by the patriarchal mythos. No longer does the creator "own" the creature. Instead, at least one type of creature, humankind, has assumed responsibility for its own existence—and as we read the poem we cannot help but think that this change is all to the good. Eve's rebellion against Adam's authority is similarly "fruitful." Eve ruptures the divinely ordained relationship of male dominance and female submission. But then she takes the initiative (just as she had earlier taken the initiative in the primal sin itself) in recreating their relationship on a level of equality. At the end of book 10, Adam and Eve kneel together in mutual forgiveness and common repentance, and the final image we receive of Adam and Eve seems to imply that, created unequal, they have made themselves equals:

> The world was all before them, where to choose
> Their place of rest, and Providence their guide:
> They hand in hand, with wand'ring steps and slow,
> Through Eden took their solitary way.
>
> [*PL* 12.646–49]

The suggestions in *Paradise Lost* that resistance to authority may be a good thing are latent rather than overt, but they are sufficiently strong to create a "counter-poem" that works beneath the surface of Milton's "official" justification of God's ways to man. It is this counter-poem that the Romantics, including Mary Shelley, sought to "rescue" by stripping away the patriarchal mythos in which Milton had buried his kernel of truth—the truth that all human beings are (or should be) free and equal. Exactly how Mary Shelley achieves this goal will be the subject of the next sections of this essay.[16]

## III

Mary Shelley's desire to disentangle Milton's "counter-poem" is first demonstrated by the passage she chooses for her epigraph:

> Did I request thee, Maker, from my clay
> To mold me man, did I solicit thee
> From darkness to promote me?
>
> [*PL* 10.743–45]

Adam's anguished question to his maker remains, in *Paradise Lost,* unanswered. Brought into being without his request or consent, Adam has been commanded to love and obey his creator. Summoned to play a game governed by rules (all of them set by God) he does not understand, Adam is now to be punished for breaking these rules. Is not there something a little cruel about a God who creates in human beings the capacity to sin, and who foreknows that they will sin, but who nevertheless insists on punishing them when they do sin? This is the question that Adam's plaint raises. But in *Paradise Lost* this moment of brutal understanding quickly passes. Adam himself reasons his way from accusation of God to self-accusation, and beyond self-accusation to (with the help of Eve) repentance. Yet by abstracting this moment out of context, and by elaborating Adam's accusatory question into an entire novel, Mary Shelley forces us to confront the possibility that the creator (i.e., the patriarchal creator as envisioned in the Judeo-Christian mythos, and as poetically portrayed in Milton's poem) is at best incompetent, and at worst a cruel sadist. The possibility that the real object of Mary Shelley's bitterness is God himself seems to make many commentators on *Frankenstein* acutely nervous. Tannenbaum, for example, denies any significant similarity between Frankenstein and Milton's God: "Frankenstein approaches Milton's God only in terms of the characteristic that the Satanist view of *Paradise Lost* most frequently attributes to him, his vindictive nature."[17] Yet the monster's response to *Paradise Lost* suggests a far broader similarity between God and Frankenstein:

> But *Paradise Lost* excited different and far deeper emotions. I read it as I had read the other volumes which had fallen into my hands, as a true history. It moved every feeling of wonder and awe that the picture of an omnipotent God warring with his creatures was capable of exciting. I often referred the several situations, as their similarity struck me, to my own. Like Adam, I was apparently united by no link to any other being in existence; but his state was far different from mine in every other respect. He had come forth from the hands of God a perfect creature, happy and prosperous, guarded by the especial care of his Creator; he was allowed to converse with and acquire knowledge from beings of a superior nature, but I was wretched, helpless, and alone. Many times I considered Satan as the fitter emblem of my condition, for often, like him, when I viewed the bliss of my protectors, the bitter gall of envy rose within me.[18]

What Satan and Adam have principally in common is their status as secondary, created beings—creatures who at least in theory owe gratitude and obedience to their creator. In absorbing into himself the qualities of both Adam and Satan, the Monster becomes the universal embodiment of the creature. Standing over against him, as creator, is Frankenstein, just as Milton's God stands over against the entire created universe. Can the ways of the creator toward the creature be justified? This is the question Milton poses in *Paradise Lost*. His "official," "public" answer is yes. But, as we have seen, the Romantics detected in *Paradise Lost* a half-suppressed countervoice which, rather than putting man on trial before the bar of God's justice, instead hungered to put God on trial before man's idea of justice. In *Frankenstein* Mary Shelley does what Milton, in the eyes of the Romantics, wanted but did not dare to do: she puts the patriarchal creator on trial, and she finds him guilty. That is, she works through the possibility that the creator's ways toward the creature are not and cannot possibly be just—that whatever justice may exist in the universe is created not by God but by humankind as we assume collective responsibility for our own destiny.

The most significant similarity between God and Victor Frankenstein is their common status as "male mothers." Victor Frankenstein gives birth to his creature without any sort of assistance from a woman. As we have already seen, a similar pattern of "male motherhood" is at work within *Paradise Lost:* God, Satan, and Adam all "give birth" in the course of Milton's poem. Simply because Milton's myths are all more or less "orthodox," we may well read *Paradise Lost* without sensing anything perverse in the poem's insistence that the ability to create new life is a power possessed exclusively by males. But if we read *Paradise Lost* "through" *Frankenstein,* then the central position that "male motherhood"occupies in Milton's poem (and, of course, also in the Judeo-Christian myths upon which he draws) becomes apparent. (I might as well confess that I am here talking about myself. I studied and taught *Paradise Lost* for years without ever seeing anything the least unusual in Milton's view of creation. But a reading of *Frankenstein* instantly and radically changed my perception of the creation myths in *Paradise Lost*.) Moreover, if we read *Paradise Lost* with Mary Shelley's parodic description of "male motherhood" fresh in our minds, we begin to sense that there is something intrinsically monstrous in this idea. That male motherhood is inherently monstrous is apparent, first, in the inability of the patriarchal creator, whether God or Frankenstein, to create the kind of being he sets out to create. The monstrous physiognomy of Victor Frankenstein's creature serves as an objective correlative of the monstrous act that brought him into existence. Here we encounter an apparent contradiction between *Paradise Lost* and *Frankenstein*. For as the Monster himself notes, God's creative labors issue in a beautiful creature, while Victor horribly botched the job:

> Accursed Creator! Why did you form a monster so hideous that even *you* turned from me in disgust? God, in pity, made man beautiful and alluring, after his own image; but my form is a filthy type of yours, more horrid even from the very resemblance. [P. 125]

Yet the contrast here may be more apparent than real, for Adam's beautiful exterior conceals a fatal flaw: a propensity toward sin that brings upon humankind untold misery. Why did God, knowing full well that sooner or later human beings would sin, create in them the capacity to sin? The events in *Paradise Lost* force us to ask this question, but neither God nor Milton will stay for an answer. Mary Shelley, less sanguine than Milton, demands an answer. And if we let ourselves read *Paradise Lost* through her eyes, we cannot help but wonder whether the male mother who gives birth to Adam is any more competent than the male mother of Mary Shelley's nameless Monster. Furthermore, Mary Shelley suggests a specific reason why male motherhood is "monstrous": it issues exclusively from the will rather than the heart.[19] Victor Frankenstein creates the Monster not out of love for the developing creature but purely out of a need to demonstrate his mastery over the process of nature. The Monster, we might say, leaps full-grown (indeed, overgrown) from the *mind* (not the loins) of his creator—like Athena from the head of Zeus, like Sin from the mind of Satan, like the Son from the mind of God, like Eve from the side of Adam. The last of these acts of birth is perhaps less monstrous than the others, because Eve at least emerges from a place in reasonable proximity to Adam's sexual organ, and because she is created out of Adam's need for a companion. But God has no "need" of the Son or of Adam, nor does Satan "need" Sin. No possibility of reciprocity exists in these cases, and thus the act of creation itself seems motivated solely by the creator's desire to possess an inferior being over whom he can exercise power. By this means Mary Shelley forces us to recognize that all these male births, insofar as they issue from motives other than love, are in varying degrees unnatural—that the true "monster" here is not the creature but his creator.

If the motives that impel God and Frankenstein to bring their creatures into existence are similar, so too are the ways in which they behave toward their creatures. To both creators the act of creation entails a descent from the spiritual toward the material. Milton's God is pure light, while Adam and Eve are creatures of flesh and blood. Why is God willing to let his "image" be degraded by this entrance into matter? Even Milton has difficulty answering this question: at one point Raphael speculates Neoplatonically that perhaps God will someday allow the human soul to ascend from the material prison in which it is entrapped, and this notion seems to imply that the very creation of the material world was in some sense a "fall." In any case, between a purely spiritual God and his material creature a great gulf is fixed. The creature is by his very nature an "other," eternally standing over against a creator whose nature is fundamentally different from (and immeasurably superior to) the nature of the creature. Between Frankenstein and his creature there is a similar gulf. Victor "dreams" his creature. But when this dream stands over against him in inescapably physical form, he is appalled by the incommensurability between his spirit and this gross body:

> I had worked hard for nearly two years, for the sole purpose of infusing life into an inanimate body. For this I had deprived myself of rest and health. I had desired it with an ardour that far exceeded moderation; but now that I had finished, the beauty of the dream vanished, and breathless horror and disgust filled my heart. [P. 56]

Both God and Frankenstein also "abandon" their creatures. Victor's refusal to take responsibility for his "child" is obvious: he takes one look at what he has created and flees. God's abandonment of Adam and Eve is less obvious, for both Milton and his sources want to "justify" God's behavior. Yet the skeptical reader cannot help but notice that God, knowing full well that Adam and Eve have a propensity toward sin, nevertheless leaves them to their own devices—with the unsurprising consequence that they do in fact sin. And the similarity between God and Frankenstein extends one step further yet. Having created a helpless and flawed creature and having then abandoned this creature in disgust, Frankenstein nevertheless insists upon holding the Monster morally accountable for all the crimes he commits in his desperate attempts to claim from his parent the self that has been denied him. So too God, having created in Adam and Eve a propensity to sin, and foreknowing that they will sin, nevertheless holds both them and their descendants solely accountable for the consequences of their sin. Indeed, both God and Frankenstein place their creatures in an intolerable and insoluble double bind. Denied the knowledge that would enable them to choose responsibly, Adam and Eve and their descendants are nevertheless held accountable by God for the consequences of their sins, just as Frankenstein holds the Monster responsible for the murders of William, Clerval, and Elizabeth. In both instances the creature, launched upon the world as a "free" being with the power to shape his own destiny, is nevertheless expected to do nothing contrary to the will of his creator. The creature is in fact simultaneously an autonomous self and an extension of his creator, and these two dimensions of his existence are absolutely incompatible. Caught in this dilemma, the creature twists and turns. And this dilemma is, Mary Shelley reveals to us, the dilemma of patriarchy itself. The patriarchal creator is driven to create by the will to exercise authority over his Other, and yet as long as he sees the Other as merely an extension of himself he and his creature remain locked in a sterile combat. Is there a way out of this dilemma? Mary Shelley, I believe, thought so, and in the next section of this essay I shall seek to elucidate her alternative to patriarchy.

## IV

Jacques Derrida has taught us that in any text the absences are no less eloquent than the presences, the unspoken at least as important as the spoken.[20] In *Frankenstein* (and in the shadowy *Paradise Lost* that looms through Frankenstein) the principal absence is the mother, the generative female who might offer an alternative to the patriarchal creator. A good many critics have noted that in *Frankenstein* the female reproductive power has been displaced. Robert Kiely, for example, sees in *Frankenstein* a moral drama in which the deaths of William, Clerval, and Elizabeth serve to punish Victor for his attempt to "usurp the power of women":

In describing the way in which Frankenstein's experiment seems most "unnatural," Mary Shelley implies a definition of the natural which is peculiarly feminine in bias. For her, Frankenstein's presumption is not in his attempt to usurp the power of the gods—she quite willingly grants him his "divine" attributes—but in his attempt to usurp the power of women.[21]

U. C. Knoepflmacher sees *Frankenstein* as "a novel of omnipresent fathers and absent mothers," in which the motive energy comes from Mary Shelley's hunger for the mother she never had and from her powerfully ambivalent feelings toward her father.[22] And Kate Ellis finds in *Frankenstein* an implied critique of the male who attempts to create new life without benefit of copulation:

> *Frankenstein* is indeed a birth myth, but one in which the parent who "brought death into the world, and all our woe" is not a woman but a man who has pushed the masculine prerogative past the limits of nature, creating life not through the female body but in a laboratory.[23]

If the "horror" of this book arises in part from Frankenstein's unnatural usurpation of the prerogatives of woman, then this horror is compounded by the systematic elimination from the novel of all women who might potentially assert the claims of the generative female. Frankenstein's mother dies just before he leaves for the university. The servant Justine, who fills the place of a mother in the lives of Victor's younger siblings,[24] is hanged for the supposed murder of William, and Victor's beloved Elizabeth dies at the hands of the Monster a few hours after her marriage to Frankenstein. All these deaths, the last in particular, suggest that the exigencies of Mary Shelley's fable demand the exclusion from the novel of the genitally and generatively potent female. No less important in this respect is a female who, rather than dying, is never born: the female Monster that Victor Frankenstein first agrees to create and then refuses to create. Indeed, Frankenstein's refusal is in some ways the pivotal moment of the plot. Milton's God, faced by Adam's request for a mate, accedes, and the creation of Eve initiates the "countermovement" within *Paradise Lost*—a movement away from hierarchy and obedience toward freedom and equality. No similar countermovement occurs within Mary Shelley's grotesque parody of *Paradise Lost,* and this difference between the two texts seems to me no less significant than the similarities noted above. The generative female succeeds in subverting the hierarchical perfection of Milton's patriarchal cosmos, and as a consequence the poem can end in a vision of fruition and hope. But no similar rupture occurs in *Franken-stein,* simply because the creator here refuses to allow the female to exist. As a consequence, the sterile struggle between the patriarchal creator and his creature must here proceed to its terrible end.

Some recent theoretical proposals by Alexander Greimas and Fredric Jameson offer a useful way of explaining why the absence of the generative female is of central importance to *Frankenstein.*[25] Greimas has proposed that "signification" emerges out of the relationship among four variables: the explicit "signifier" and three implied terms—the "opposite" of the signifier, the "negation" of the signifier, and the "negation of the opposite." These relations can be diagramed as follows, with "S" representing the Signifier:

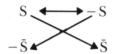

Jameson explains this diagram as follows:

> If, using Greimas' convenient example, we take S to be the marriage rule of a given society, the semantic rectangle allows us to generate a complete table or inventory of the sexual conventions or possibilities of the society in question. So −S may be read as a symbol for those sexual relationships which are proscribed or considered abnormal (e.g., incest), while the simple negative S̄ stands for those relationships which are not matrimonial, i.e., not prescribed or legalized by the marriage system in force: these would be, for instance, adultery on the woman's part. The fourth term −S̄ may then be understood as the simple negative of the abnormal, forbidden relations, or in other words those sexual relationships which are neither abnormal nor explicitly forbidden: e.g., masculine adultery.[26]

"The . . . merit of Greimas' mechanism," Jameson adds, "is to enjoin upon us the obligation to articulate any apparently static free-standing concept or term into that binary opposition which it structurally presupposes and which forms the very basis for its intelligibility." And Jameson also makes an important addition to Greimas's model: "In actual practice . . . it frequently turns out that we are able to articulate a given concept into only three of the four available positions; the final one, $-\bar{S}$, remains a cipher or an enigma for the mind." "At this point," Jameson adds, "the development of the model . . . may take the form of a search for the missing term . . . , which we may now identify as none other than the 'negation of the negation' familiar from dialectical philosophy. It is, indeed, because the negation of a negation is such a decisive leap, such a production or generation of new meaning, that we so frequently come upon a system in the incomplete state shown above (only three terms out of four given). Under such circumstances the negation of the negation then becomes the primary work which the mechanism is called upon to accomplish."[27] I find it useful to apply this model to *Frankenstein,* as follows:

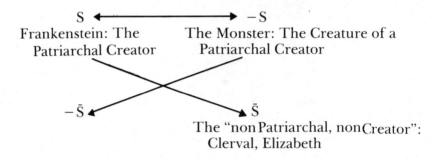

The fourth term here is ostentatiously missing from Mary Shelley's text, but the "semantic rectangle" of Greimas and Jameson allows us to locate this missing term as the nonmale, noncreature, nonobject, as, in other words, the creative, female *subject.* The discovery of this "negation of the negation" is, I believe, the "primary work" in which Mary Shelley is here engaged. *Frankenstein* strains to bring into being this missing term, the generative, nonpatriarchal creator—free of all dependence upon an exterior creator, freely creating in her own right, and claiming no residual rights of possession over the beings she creates. In pointing beyond itself to this possibility of freedom and creativity, *Frankenstein* opens up to us a new awareness of our birthright—a birthright we have as yet scarcely begun to make our own.

The semantic rectangle makes it clear that a resolution to the destructive effects of patriarchy must involve a liberation of a power which is, under patriarchy, suppressed: the power of free, unpossessive creation. For Mary Shelley, this power is, in the current order of things (i.e., in a society which demands that men be "masterful"), found primarily in women—although as we shall see this power is not restricted to women. The mother whose absence from *Frankenstein* speaks to us so eloquently is the principal exemplar of the creative power. Indeed she is a Trojan Horse within the bastion of patriarchy, for her concern with the organic growth of the child can counterbalance the patriarch's demand for obedience. Scattered through *Frankenstein* are several images of nutritive parent/child relationship. Invariably these nutritive families include both a father and a mother. An important example is Frankenstein's own family during his early years:

> My mother's tender caresses and my father's smile of benevolent pleasure while regarding me are my first recollections. I was their plaything and their idol, and something better—their child, the innocent and helpless creature bestowed on them by heaven, whom to bring up to good, and whose future lot it was in their hands to direct to happiness or misery, according as they fulfilled their duties towards me. With this deep consciousness of what they owed towards the being to which they had given life, added to the active spirit of tenderness that animated both, it may be imagined that while during every hour of my infant life I received a lesson of patience, of charity, and of self-control, I was so guided by a silken cord that all seemed but one train of enjoyment to me. [P. 33]

And while he is living in the DeLacey's shed, the Monster develops a similar image of the "normal" family:

> I heard of the difference of sexes, and the birth and growth of children, how the father doted on the smiles of the infant, and the lively sallies of the older child, how all the life and cares of the mother were wrapped up in the precious charge, how the mind of youth expanded and gained knowledge, of brother, sister, and all the various relationships which bind one human being to another in mutual bonds. [P. 115]

What the mother brings to the family, it would appear, is a concern for the child not as possession, as object, but rather as an emergent, autonomous self. In the "normal" family, the mother's nutritive concern for the child can in practice counterbalance the theoretically absolute rights of the father. But if the mother is removed from the family, the patriarchal social structure that reduces the child to the status of object reasserts itself—and the struggle between Frankenstein and his Monster graphically demonstrates the consequences. The alternative to patriarchy, it should now therefore be clear, is not matriarchy: the substitution of the powerful, controlling female for the powerful, controlling male. For if woman too creates only in order to possess her creation, she loses the very quality that establishes her as an alternative to the patriarch: her willingness (a willingness we cannot find either in God or in Frankenstein) to nurture her creatures as long as they need nurture, and to let them go (again unlike the patriarchal creator) when they are ready to assume responsibility for their own lives. Nor are the qualities that define the mother as an alternative to the patriarch generically female. After he gives birth to his Monster, Frankenstein experiences an episode of brain fever. Henry Clerval nurses Victor through this illness, becoming in effect a kind of surrogate "mother" (in a positive sense of the word this time) who gives new life to his friend:

> Clerval called forth the better feelings of my heart; he again taught me to love the aspect of nature and the cheerful faces of children. Excellent friend! How sincerely did you love me and endeavour to elevate my mind until it was on a level with your own! A selfish pursuit had cramped and narrowed me until your gentleness and affection warmed and opened my senses; I became the same happy creature who, a few years ago, loved and beloved by all, had no sorrow or care. [P. 68]

Clerval can nourish and regenerate Victor because he and Victor perceive each other as equals. As Mary Wollstonecraft insisted, the key to a nutritive relationship between two human beings (whether these individuals are male or female is irrelevant) is a mutual respect for the independence, the selfhood, the "subjecthood" of the other. So too the good parent sees her/his child from the beginning as a person, not as a possession. Patriarchy denies the possibility of mutual relationships between equals, demanding instead that in every human relationship one person must be the master while the other must be a slave, that one must give orders while the other obeys, that one must be a subject while the other is an object. It is this system of patriarchy—not John Milton or William Godwin or Percy Shelley or any other individual male—that Mary Shelley here summons to the bar of judgment—and finds guilty.

V

The overriding theme of *Frankenstein*, I have here argued, is patriarchy, which I can now finally define as a *social and psychological structure that defines the creature as Other, as object, inherently inferior to and therefore the rightful possession of the creating male subject.* On the one hand, the word *patriarchy* denotes an archaic social formation, in which the woman's reproductive capacity is literally owned by the male. In this sense patriarchy is, as Sheila Rowbotham notes, a precapitalist social formation:

> The sexual division of labour and the possession of women by men predates capitalism. Patriarchal authority is based on male control over the woman's productive capacity, and over her person. This control existed before the development of capitalist commodity production. It belonged to a society in which the persons of human beings were owned by others. Patriarchy, however, is contradicted by the dominant mode of production in capitalism because in capitalism the owner of capital owns and controls the labour power but not the persons of his labourers.[28]

In various ways bourgeois society has systematically eroded the structures of patriarchy. The great bourgeois novels of the nineteenth century offer numerous models of sons who successfully rebel against their fathers to win independent identities, and bourgeois society has also at least partly accommodated itself to Mary Wollstonecraft's prophetic demand that women should be legally and socially the equals of men. In summoning patriarchy to the bar of judgment, therefore, Mary Shelley was in one respect serving as a spokesperson for an emergent bourgeoisie, eager to strip away the last traces of feudal oppression by asserting the claims of the free, autonomous subject. Yet the psychology of patriarchy tends to persist under capitalism—indeed, it plays a crucial role in legitimating capitalist institutions. If the feudal baron sees his son and heir as an extension of himself, the baron of industry claims to have produced single handedly not only his sons but "his" factories, railroads, etcetera, and because he believes that he created these instruments of commodity production, he also claims rights of ownership over them. Indeed bourgeois society, far from abolishing the category of the creature (the Other, the object) has, as Marx revealed, transformed all workers into creatures of the one great subject, capital itself. Beginning in an attack on patriarchy conducted in the name of individual liberty, bourgeois society has ended by recreating patriarchy in a new form. And since the revolutionary thrust of *Frankenstein* is directed not at feudal social structures per se but rather at the process (a process that continues under capitalism) by which the Other, the object, is generated, the book retains its *energeia* even today. Only a few years before Mary Shelley wrote *Frankenstein,* Hegel worked out his analysis of the master/slave dialectic, in the full expectation that during his lifetime this dialectic would resolve itself within the utopia of the Prussian state. But oppression did not pass from the earth in Hegel's lifetime; rather, at that moment the master/slave dialectic began to assume a new form, as the bourgeoisie confronted the proletariat. Hegel's concept of the master/slave dialectic therefore remains a powerful tool of social analysis, even though the feudal social structure that prompted Hegel to develop this concept has passed away. Furthermore, the passage in the *Phenomenology* in which Hegel develops this concept continues to exercise a prophetic power over us, simply because Hegel here demands that we look beyond the oppression and inequality of society (whether feudal or bourgeois) as it exists, toward a utopian world in which no one will be a master, because no one will be a slave. *Frankenstein,* I would propose, works upon us in much the same way. The novel dramatizes for us not merely one specific manifestation of the master/slave dialectic but rather the operations of this dialectic itself. Mary Shelley gives us, in Victor Frankenstein, an inflexible, impacable image of the master, who can see his creature only as a slave, as Other, as object. But she has also here given voice to the Other itself, as we follow the Monster's groping movements into consciousness, into language, into selfhood. And in working through to its disastrous end the struggle between the two, she has also at least implicitly pointed beyond the sterile struggle of master and slave toward an alternative world of equality and cooperation.

In the book the struggle of the Other toward the reclamation of its birthright is futile, and Mary Shelley reveals not only the anguish of the Other but the reasons why the struggles of the Other toward liberation here end in failure. The problem is that the Monster continues to look beyond himself for an identity and therefore remains dependent upon his creator. The Monster demands that his creator either give him the self he lacks or give him an Other of his own so that he can become autonomous. But Frankenstein refuses both these demands. Thus the Monster remains to the end both nameless and wifeless. In a desperate attempt to capture an identity, the Monster kills his creator's younger brother (compare Satan's decision to seduce Adam and Eve, after he decides that an attack on God himself would be futile), and then his best friend, and then his wife, and finally the creator himself. In each case the Monster is apparently attempting to become the person he kills, but, unsurprisingly, none of these crimes wins for the Monster the love of his creator, and so his attempts to win an identity end in frustration. As a consequence the exultant cry of the object discovering its freedom sounds, in *Frankenstein*, at best only faintly. Instead we hear the creature's anguished cry of protest against an indifferent creator. It may therefore seem that the revolutionary possibilities inherent in Mary Shelley's myth remain only half developed. But we must remember that when Mary Shelley wrote *Frankenstein* the revolutionary surge unleashed by the French Revolution was in retreat. It is therefore not surprising that the emphasis in *Frankenstein* should fall on protest against tyranny (the tyranny of the patriarchal mythos over consciousness, the tyranny of men over women, the tyranny of the bourgeois subject over its Other) rather than on the hope of liberation. I would also argue that Mary Shelley's refusal to proclaim the freedom of the Other is in fact one of the strengths of her book. Nowhere in Mary Shelley do we find that tendency, common among many writers (Percy Shelley not least), to assume that a verbal declaration of freedom suffices to break the bonds of tyranny. Mary Shelley recognizes that a premature declaration of the end of tyranny can blind us to the ways in which traditional institutions and habits of thought control our lives, and therefore she devotes herself to unmasking the effects of such social institutions and mental habits on our action rather than to proclaiming a new order. And despite Mary Shelley's reluctance to make premature proclamations of an end to tyranny, I would still see *Frankenstein* as an important breakthrough in human consciousness. No text of the time so fully integrates the feminist consciousness pioneered by Mary Wollstonecraft and the political radicalism of William Godwin. Indeed, not until the emergent socialism of the 1880s will we again find a feminist critique of male dominance broadening into a rigorous analysis of the poisonous influence that authority and hierarchy exercise over all social relationships. Even in our own time *Frankenstein* continues to challenge the assumptions both of those male revolutionaries who refuse to see the pervasive influence on all of us of patriarchal habits of thought, and of those feminists who refuse to recognize that the oppression of women is a consequence not of the perversity of individual men but rather of a social structure that pits rulers against the ruled, capital against labor, managers against workers, the propertied against the propertyless, owners against producers. In the end the only true "negation of the negation" is a classless society, a society in which the category of the Other, the object, dissolves, giving way to a world in which the free development of each is a necessary condition of the free development of all. In our struggle toward such a society Mary Shelley is, as I have here attempted to show, one of our allies. And so too is John Milton, because he elevated the patriarchal mythos into consciousness, and because he took the first tentative steps toward the critique of patriarchy—a critique which Mary Shelley and the other Romantics continued and expanded, but which has not yet been brought to completion. Almost 160 years separate *Paradise Lost* from *Frankenstein;* another 160 years separate Mary Shelley from us. Clearly, the eradication of patriarchy is a long and painful process. Yet a common commitment to human liberation links John Milton to Mary Shelley, and together they define for us a tradition that is ours to inherit, if we have the courage.[29]

## Notes

1. C. S. Lewis, *A Preface* to Paradise Lost (London: Oxford University Press, 1942), p. 78. For Bush's view of Milton, see Douglas Bush, *English Literature in the Earlier Seventeenth Century, 1600–1660*, 2d ed. (Oxford: Clarendon Press, 1962), pp. 377–424.

2. See in particular Lee Sterrenburg, "Mary Shelley's Monster: Politics and Psyche in *Frankenstein*," in *The Endurance of Frankenstein*, ed. George Levine and U. C. Knoepflmacher (Berkeley: University of California Press, 1979), pp. 143–71. See also Sylvia Bowerbank, "The Social Order vs. the Wretch: Mary Shelley's Contradictory-mindedness in *Frankenstein*," *Journal of English Literary History* 46 (1979): 418–31. "Unlike Shelley," Bowerbank argues, "Mary was imbued with the spirit of conservatism which dominated England during her adolescence" (p. 418). However, Bowerbank presents little evidence to support this assertion. The advocates of the theory that Mary Shelley's social views were conservative are wont to quote a passage from her Journal:

In the first place, with regard to "the good cause"—the cause of the advancement of freedom and knowledge, of the rights of women, &c.—I am not a person of opinions.

I have said elsewhere that human beings differ greatly in this. Some have a passion
for reforming the world; others do not cling to particular opinions. That my parents
and Shelley were of the former class, make me respect it. I respect such when joined
to real disinterestedness, toleration, and a clear understanding. . . . For myself, I
earnestly desire the good and enlightenment of my fellow-creatures, and see all, in
the present course, tending to the same, and rejoice; but I am not for violent ex-
tremes, which only bring on an injurious reaction.

See *Mary Shelley's Journal,* ed. Frederick L. Jones (Norman, Okla.: University of Ok-
lahoma Press, 1947), p. 204. On this subject I would note that a great many years
separate the nineteen-year-old woman who wrote *Frankenstein* from the forty-one-year-
old woman who wrote this journal passage. I would also point out that the quoted
passage in no way implies a preference for conservative over radical political views.
Rather the subject of the passage is Mary Shelley's distrust of *all* varieties of dogmatism.
Insofar as the author of this passage displays a preference for one kind of political
attitude over another, she clearly favors the apostles of progress (if tempered by "toleration") over their opponents, and the subject of the passage is, not Mary Shelley's
opposition to social change, but her reluctance to speak out on social issues. The
passage thus offers no real evidence that the adult Mary Shelley had adopted conservative political views.

3. Leslie Tannenbaum, "From Filthy Type to Truth: Miltonic Myth in *Frankenstein,*"
*Keats-Shelley Journal* 26 (1977): 101–13.

4. Sandra M. Gilbert and Susan Gubar, *The Madwoman in the Attic* (New Haven,
Conn.: Yale University Press, 1979), p. 221. I classify the Gilbert-Gubar view of *Frankenstein* as a "cultural feminist" interpretation, in that they tend to see male/female
relations as static; that is, they assume that all men are by nature oppressors and that
women have no options except "despairing acquiescence" (a phrase that Gilbert and
Gubar apply to Mary Shelley) or sullen resistance. Cultural documents such as novels
become, when seen from this perspective, merely reflections of this static confrontation
of men and women. Gilbert and Gubar also tend to see literature as existing in isolation
from society. Milton's supposed "misogyny" thus becomes merely a proof that he was a
bad man, and Mary Shelley's failure to protest this misogyny becomes a sign of her
cowardice. In contrast, a Marxian interpretation of social relationships sees the forms
of male oppression and of female resistance and self-assertion as evolving in response
to changes in the social relations of production. As applied to literature, a Marxian
perspective enables us to see Milton's and Mary Shelley's views of male/female relationship as conditioned by the social realities of their times. But a Marxian perspective also
allows us to seek in literary texts signs of the emergent claims of women to full human
freedom, and I detect such signs in the writings both of Milton and of Mary Shelley.

5. My sense that *Frankenstein* encodes a powerfully subversive vision of human social
relations is shared by at least two of the contributors to *The Endurance of Frankenstein,*
Levine's and Knoepflmacher's valuable collection of critical essays on the book: see Kate
Ellis, "Monsters in the Garden: Mary Shelley and the Bourgeois Family," pp. 123–42,
and Peter Dale Scott, "Vital Artifice: Mary, Percy, and the Psychopolitical Integrity of
*Frankenstein,*" pp. 172–202. At least one other critic also shares my belief that Mary
Shelley saw Milton as primarily a proponent of human liberation: Milton A. Mays,
"*Frankenstein,* Mary Shelley's Black Theodicy," *Southern Humanities Review* 3 (Spring
1969): 146–53. Christopher Small has brilliantly reconstructed Mary Shelley's intellectual milieu in *Mary Shelley's Frankenstein: Tracing the Myth* (Pittsburgh: University of
Pittsburgh Press, 1972), and Small's general assessment of Mary Shelley's political and
social attitudes is similar to my own. However, none of these critics has focused on the

subject that is my primary concern here: Mary Shelley's response to Milton's treatment of the mythos of patriarchy.

6. Willaim Godwin, *Caleb Williams* (New York: W. W. Norton, 1977), and William Godwin, *Enquiry Concerning Political Justice*, ed. Isaac Kramnick (Baltimore, Md.: Penguin Books, 1976), esp. pp. 725–35.

7. Mary Wollstonecraft, *A Vindication of the Rights of Women*, ed. Carol H. Poston (New York: W. W. Norton, 1975).

8. Joseph A. Wittreich, Jr., introduction to *The Romantics on Milton*, ed. Wittreich (Cleveland, Ohio: Case Western Reserve University Press, 1970), p. 20.

9. Ibid., p. 35.

10. Godwin, *Enquiry*, p. 309.

11. Wollstonecraft, *A Vindication*, pp. 20–21.

12. Wittreich, *The Romantics on Milton*, p. 538.

13. Ibid., p. 531.

14. U. C. Knoepflmacher, "Thoughts on the Aggression of Daughters," in *The Endurance of Frankenstein*, pp. 88–119.

15. All quotations from *Paradise Lost* are from *The Complete Poetical Works of Milton*, ed. Douglas Bush (Boston: Houghton Mifflin, 1965). References will be by book and line number and will be included in the text.

16. At least a few modern critics share my belief that the Romantics were not entirely deluded when they detected a certain ambivalence in Milton's treatment of obedience versus disobedience: see, for example, Lawrence W. Hyman, *The Quarrel Within* (Port Washington, N.Y.: Kennikat Press, 1972), pp. 34–55.

17. Tannenbaum, "From Filthy Type to Truth," p. 110.

18. Mary Shelley, *Frankenstein* (New York: New American Library, 1965), p. 124. All references to *Frankenstein* will be to this edition and will be incorporated into my text. I use this edition rather than the widely used edition of James Rieger because the New American Library edition includes the revisions Mary Shelley made for the second edition. Rieger prefers the first edition for one reason only. He believes that Percy Shelley is virtually the "co-author" of the novel, and therefore the first edition is presumably closer to—not Mary's—but Percy's intention than is the revised edition Mary published after her husband's death. But I see *Frankenstein* as Mary Shelley's novel from beginning to end, and therefore I prefer the second edition to the first in that it represents her most fully considered intentions.

19. For some useful comments on *Frankenstein* as a dramatization of the struggle between willful egoism and human sympathy, see Robert Kiely, *The Romantic Novel in England* (Cambridge, Mass.: Harvard University Press, 1972), esp. pp. 166ff.

20. See, for example, Jacques Derrida, "Difference," in *Speech and Phenomena*, ed. and trans. David B. Allison (Evanston, Ill.: Northwestern University Press, 1973), pp. 129–60.

21. Kiely, *The Romantic Novel*, p. 164.

22. Knoepflmacher, *The Endurance of Frankenstein*, p. 90.

23. Ellis, "Monsters in the Garden," p. 142. On this subject see also Irving H. Buchen, "*Frankenstein* and the Alchemy of Creation and Evolution," *Wordsworth Circle* 8 (1977): 103–12.

24. "[Justine] was warmly attached to the child who is now dead and acted towards him like a most affectionate mother" (p. 81).

25. I rely on Jameson's summary of Greimas's theory in *The Prison-House of Language* (Princeton, N.J.: Princeton University Press, 1972), pp. 163ff.

26. Ibid., pp. 163–64.

27. Ibid., pp. 164–67.

28. Sheila Rowbotham, *Woman's Consciousness, Man's World* (Baltimore, Md.: Penguin Books, 1973), p. 117.

29. An earlier version of this paper was presented at the 1979 MLA Convention as part of a special session on Marxist Approaches to Fantasy and Romance organized by Abdul Jan Mohamed. In revising the paper I have profited from comments by my fellow panelists Michael McKeon and Eileen Sypher.

# Hermeneutics from Gadamer to Poeggeler

## Algis Mickunas

### Ohio University

THE term *hermeneutics* was coined in the seventeenth century. Its Greek cognates cover a wide field. In the *Epinomis* to Plato's Laws we find a discussion of arts, one of which is the hermeneutical; it illuminates the cryptic sayings of gods without making any claims to truth. In Aristotle's *Organon, peri hermeneias* is one mode of speaking. Subsequently hermeneutics was developed into an auxiliary discipline of philosophy, theology, and jurisprudence, and equipped with specific rules for the explication of texts.[1]

Hermeneutics passed through the major crises of the Western tradition. It appeared in Plato's confrontation with the gods of myths and poets, and in the encounter of Hellenic allegorical thought with the Judeo-Christian historical and prophetic orientation. It was present in the efforts to transmit Greek education to the Latin world and to overcome the linguistic barrier of Latin. It was evident in the attempts to pass on to posterity Roman jurisprudence, Greek thought, and the Holy Scriptures. It reappeared in Reformation attempts to expound the Bible from within as *sui ipsius interpres.* Finally, Schlegel and Schleiermacher freed hermeneutics from its auxiliary role and expanded it into a universal theory of understanding and an exposition of meaningful objectivations of historical existence.[2]

The oldest philosophical lexicon, Rudolph Gocklenius's *Lexicon Philosophicum* (1613), has an article on hermeneutics under the Greek term *hermeneia.* It is an excellent account of *hermeneia* in medieval theology and jurisprudence, and also includes a discussion of the origins of *hermeneia* as a technical term in

48

patristic literature. Interestingly, the eight-volume *English Encyclopedia of Philosophy* (1967) has nothing to say about hermeneutics, despite the preeminence of that term throughout the philosophical tradition and in the European thought of this century.[3]

In contemporary Continental thought, hermeneutics is extended to comprehend a foundational philosophy of human studies as a whole. It includes not only philology but also all areas of scientific endeavor dealing with human beings: psychology, sociology, arts, religion, history, economics, and even the procedures of the "strict" sciences insofar as they require and assume human understanding. All sciences presuppose an initial understanding of the world and its various domains before they investigate a specific field in terms of explanatory models. Such broader understanding provides the basis for scientific work and for the interpretation of its results. The exposition of this understanding and the "prejudgments" contained within it is the task of hermeneutics. Although many contemporary thinkers are engaged in hermeneutical investigations, the present paper will discuss those contributions which extend, rather than repeat, one another. The criterion of unique contributions to the field of hermeneutics singles out the thinkers who are considered to be the outstanding contemporary representatives of the hermeneutical mode of philosophizing.

## Gadamer

The Gadamerian hermeneutics rests on Heidegger's exposition of the "hidden" presuppositions of the meaning of being that had dominated the "destiny" of the Western tradition. In this sense Heidegger's hermeneutics could be called "hermeneutics of the latent." He claims that underlying the various ontologies of the sciences and humanities there is a singular mode of interpreting Being. Despite their differences, idealism, realism, rationalism, and empiricism, are all founded on the interpretation of Being as substantive and entitative that produces the logic of essential predication and definition. The question this interpretation of Being asks is, What is something? What something is, is given in a definition, *de-finis*, a finality of the defining statement ruled by the logic of "either/or." Something is either this or not this. All scientific

and humanistic questions are founded on an uncritical acceptance of this fundamental hermeneutics of Being. It carries la-
tently all our endeavors. According to Heidegger, this interpretation of Being led Aristotle to select among the various
expressions the ones that could be either true or false, and
hence to a distinction between *apophantics* and hermeneutics. A
true expression would allow something to appear as it is in its
essence, in its whatness. This "as" is called by Heidegger
"apophantic."[4] But according to him, it abstracts the expression
from the dynamics of a situation within which the expression
functions. Hermeneutics is precisely the process of linguistic
articulation and understanding of the situation or the context.
This means that the apophantic expressions must be located in
the context of linguisticality and understanding from which the
expressions emerge and in terms of which they are interpret-
able. In this sense, the hermeneutical dimension, consisting of a
dynamic process of speaking and understanding, is much
broader and more fundamental than any of its abstract moments, such as apophantic expressions.

Following Heidegger, Gadamer attempts to expand Heidegger's work by bringing it to bear on concrete historical-
philological investigations of hermeneutical contexts and the
various presuppositions they contain.[5] For Gadamer the task of
hermeneutics is to reveal understanding as a basic modality of
human historical existence. Since understanding is articulated
linguistically, and since the individual is always immersed in the
language of his/her historical epoch, language surpasses all
individual attempts at a complete mastery of the historical
depth of linguistic meanings. In this sense language is more
than an individual could objectify for his/her scientific purposes and daily needs. It is rather an embodiment of a historical
tradition. The various objectified modes of analysis of linguistic
structures and scientific procedures comprise moments within
the historically pregiven linguistic understanding that provides
an encompassing and fluid background for various interpretations of such structures and procedures. This background
understanding, this hermeneutical dimension, surpasses the individual scientific and linguistic constructs and at the same time
allows for the interpretive understanding of such constructs
within a historical process of linguistic articulation.

According to Gadamer, today it is no longer possible to begin with mere metaphysics or epistemology. It is necessary to reflect upon language and history to reveal and explicate the presuppositions they contain. It is impossible, in principle, to begin without presuppositions, precisely because the linguistically transmitted historical understanding, within whose fluidum we live, surpasses our individual linguistic range of understanding and constitutes the open horizons of our past and future which we can never encompass. Hence this historically transmitted hermeneutics is for us more being than consciousness; it has an authority and a compelling force in our own interpretation of the world. It comprises what Gadamer calls a "historically effective consiousness" *(wirkungsgeschichtliche Bewusstsein)* that "floods" over our individual and even our social consciousness.[6] Our own experience, our consciousness with its horizons of past and future, merge with those of the historical hermeneutics to the extent that we cannot extricate ourselves from its breadth. The mergence of our horizons with those of our tradition *(Horizontverschmeltzung)* extends the historically effective consciousness to include individuals and their contributions.[7]

This aspect of Gadamerian hermeneutics must not be confused with historicism, i.e., with the claim that our historical past somehow dominates us completely with its accumulated linguistic understanding. While living in and using a language, we are not aware of its history and its temporal accumulation of meanings. Rather, it is present to us with its open horizons with which our awareness fuses. The presence of a tradition is the historically effective consciousness that does not orient the individual toward the past but provides a superfluity of hermeneutical understanding which in its depth extends in all directions and hence continuously expands our experience. It does something to us that we could not do as individuals. As Gadamer points out, "it is not what we do, not what we ought to do, but what happens beyond our doing and wanting that is here at issue."[8] Our understanding is thus a fusion into the inexhaustible depth of the hermeneutical dimension.

The hermeneutical understanding assumes the following structure in philological researches. Any given text must be located within the hermeneutical understanding from which such a text has emerged and within whose horizons it has fused. At the same time the philologist is also within his/her hermeneutical context and the horizons of his/her tradition. The philologist must be cognizant both of the text and its linguistically understood tradition and of his/her own tradition with its horizons and prejudgments. The fundamental condition for the understanding of the text is that the text and the philologist belong to the same linguistic tradition, to the same background understanding in which both the text and the philologist are partial aspects. The individual text and the philological exposition are finite and are mediated through the hermeneutical understanding with its indefinite horizons. Both have prejudgments that are deeper than their singular geneses. Since the prejudgments are embodied in language, they remain anonymous because language is not an object of experience but the medium in terms of which the world is articulated and made apparent in experience.[9] Even if we reflect on a particular prejudgment given in language, we cannot abolish it; rather our experience of the world continues to be structured by it. For example, while we are aware of a particular interpretation of Being, viz. substantive, our experience and articulation of the world continue to be structured by this prejudgment. Since the prejudgment is a part of our linguistic understanding, our mode of interpreting the world, it cannot be abolished. According to Gadamer, this means that since the consciousness which reflects upon the prejudgments and presuppositions and the historically effective consciousness constitute a fusion of horizons, the prejudgments cannot be completely surpassed: they can only be recognized.[10]

The prejudgments seem to constitute an authority of a tradition and at the same time a legitimation of a tradition from which we cannot escape. Jürgen Habermas, in fact, contends that this is Gadamer's position.[11] The historically effective consciousness seems to assume a quasi-naturalistic force. To counter this charge, Gadamer argues for a difference between compulsive and rational authority. For example, the acceptance of the classical tradition and its well-argued truths is a submission not to a quasi-naturalistic force but to a rational argument and critical reflection. In this sense the legitimating authority and its prejudgments, comprising an aspect of hermeneutical understanding, belong to the hermeneutical process itself, which can reveal the prejudgments and evaluate their range of validity without abolishing them. According to Gadamer, there is no knowledge without prejudgments. The only alternative that is left is the rejection of one prejudgment in favor of another.[12]

Human understanding is immersed in a historically effective consciousness, allowing the manifestation of individual and historical prejudgments. Yet no reflection can encompass the historically effective consciousness as a basic hermeneutical understanding. In this sense, no scientific explanation can give an exhaustive account of such an understanding. A science is a reflective process and comprises only a partial aspect of the historically effective consciousness. In turn, the prejudgments and the results of a science are interpreted within a language into whose horizons the scientific thought and pronouncements fuse. After all, even scientific reflection occurs in a language of a tradition, and the scientist cannot "step behind" such a language. The historically effective consciousness, as a linguistic process of understanding, is the fundamental power of mediation of all specific theoretical and pretheoretical modes of speaking and explaining. It mediates all objectified forms of linguistic structures. Nonetheless, it cannot itself be mediated by any other process. For Gadamer, the fundamental hermeneutical process, the historically effective consciousness that mediates every experience and every articulation of the world, is not mediated by anything. Hence the basic linguistic understanding is not a system of signs or a semiotic structure but the background in terms of which all such structures are mediated, understood, and articulated. This nonobjectifiable background is, for Gadamer, the basic hermeneutical process comprising the historically effective consciousness whose horizons constitute a playing field for sciences, humanities, and history.[13]

## Heintel

In his recent writings Gadamer suggests that there is an increasing danger of the subjugation of the human sciences to the model of the explanatory sciences. The scientific model employed by the physical sciences, according to most writers in hermeneutics, is technological, i.e., oriented toward the ability to shape, change, and master natural events. The technological model tells us not what nature is but what it is in terms of our instrumental interventions.[14] Erich Heintel's concern is, among other things, to decipher the prejudgments on which the modern technological interpretation of nature rests. By using hermeneutics, he contrasts two major interpretations of Being: the classical and the modern. Through such a contrast he shows the structure of the modern thought.[15]

Although there are various points of departure for the discussion of a particular prejudgment, Heintel selects the philosophical question of "accident." In the Western tradition there are two basic theories of accident, of something that has no necessity: the Aristotelian and the Kantian. All other theories are variations of these. For Aristotle, accident is an intersection of two events proceeding in terms of their own natural aims. Each event unfolds in accordance with its disposition *(dynamis)* toward what constitutes its actuality *(energeia)*. This process presupposes an end term, *entelecheia*, toward which the process aims. An intersection of two such events, where one disrupts the other from its aim, is called accident.

For Kant, what is accident or chance is what is *not* regulated by "natural" Newtonian laws. Whatever is not regulated by such laws is not necessary, is accidental or dependent on chance. In this sense all the events of which Aristotle spoke as having their natural development toward an end, are for Kant events of chance; they cannot be submitted to the laws of causal or mechanistic explanation. In brief, Kant rejects any natural unfolding of an event or an entity toward an end, since such an unfolding is not explainable in terms of mechanistic laws.

Given these two interpretations of chance or accident, and the two notions of what is necessary—an unfolding toward an end for Aristotle and an explanation by mechanical laws for Kant—Heintel claims that the classical conception was hermeneutical while the modern is explanatory.[16] This means that any conceptions of aim, growth, development, and understanding must be excluded from the modern scientific model of explanation and reduced to chance, to nonnecessity. This is the reason, according to Heintel, for the split between the sciences and the humanities. The latter can be hermeneutical and concern themselves with events that have no scientific necessity. The scientific import of hermeneutics is abolished. The modern hermeneutics is no longer the hermeneutics of nature in the Aristotelian sense because a hermeneutics reduced to the concerns of humanities and having no necessary scientific-mechanistic laws cannot deal with nature, the province of physical sciences and their causal explanations through mechanistic laws. Hermeneutics is incapable of providing ex-

planatory models and hence is in no position to deal with the
physical world. Its only province consists of the accidental domain of historical processes. Moreover, nature is inaccessible to
modern hermeneutics, since experience of it is founded on a
linguistic understanding as a context of interpretation of natural events. What is nature depends on the linguistically accumulated tradition of interpretation.

Hermeneutical understanding is the foundation of the
humanities, and the mechanistic explanation is the foundation
of the sciences. According to Heintel, the reason why Gadamer
fears the loss of the humanities is inherent in the temptation for
the humanities to become "scientific."[17] To achieve scientific
status, humanities tend to reduce themselves to a mechanistic
explanatory model. This temptation is present in various attempts to explain "accidental" human phenomena in terms of
behavioral "sciences" and socioeconomic models that allow the
humanities to predict human actions in terms of the given psy-
chological-motivational and socioeconomic conditions. That
this danger is there is partially the fault of modern hermeneutics. Heintel points out that the hermeneutical movement has
locked itself into an inescapable position. The historically effective consciousness and its dominant linguistic understanding
closes all avenues capable of reflecting upon humanities and
sciences from a vantage point "outside" of them. Heintel suggests that despite its claims, hermeneutics assumes such a vantage point in order to reflect upon itself as hermeneutics in
distinction to other theoretical positions. He takes up the task
of demonstrating such a vantage point.

When hermeneutical understanding is concerned with a
scientific explanation and contrasts such an explanation with a
broader linguistic process within which the explanation is comprehensible, it assumes a position of comparison that belongs
neither to the hermeneutical understanding nor to the
scientific explanation. Although hermeneuticists have assumed
that the linguistically transmitted historically effective consciousness is the ultimate dimension of mediation of all experiences, while dealing with this consciousness the hermeneuticists
must necessarily objectify it and distance themselves from it. In
the objectification they must assume a vantage point or a difference between the hermeneutical understanding and a reflection that mediates such an understanding. This mediating
reflection is the condition for hermeneutical understanding of

itself as historical. According to Heintel, the hermeneutical understanding and the linguistic fluidum in which we live have no signs or ciphers revealing that they are transmissions of a historical tradition. They become historical only when they are mediated by reflection that designates them as historical. Such a reflection is also a condition for the conception of hermeneutics as hermeneutics in distinction from other modes of thought, such as scientific and explanatory models. The reflective distance and its differentiation of hermeneutics from other modes of thought is the mediating and differentiating condition that belongs neither to hermeneutics nor to science. Heintel thus finds that this vantage point of mediation and differentiation can be justifiably called "the transcendental difference."[18]

Another set of arguments offered by Heintel against the hermeneutical linguistic understanding as the ultimate mediation of all experiences and nature indicates that 1) the direct "living in language" does not reveal language but the world; language functions anonymously. It exhausts itself by opening up a world of things in specific ways. In this sense, to speak of a language as a medium for the manifestation of nature, and even history, is to establish implicitly a distinction between language and nature and hence to take a stance outside of language and nature, i.e., to posit a difference between language and nature. 2) To claim that the historically effective consciousness, the hermeneutical understanding, has horizons that are more extensive than our individual horizons and that the two sets of horizons fuse, is to differentiate between them and at the same time to show how they are related. Both types of horizons must be objectified from the vantage point of their difference; this is the condition without which no discussion of their fusion would make sense.[19]

According to Heintel, the transcendental difference is the condition of mediation between hermeneutical understanding and explanatory sciences, between historically effective consciousness and the individual consciousness, and between theory and its practical application. Without the vantage point of the transcendental difference, we would live in language as an animal lives in its environment; we would never know that we are in a linguistic environment.[20] For Heintel, the transcendental difference is a condition that founds our understanding of a particular historical tradition in contrast to other traditions. Since hermeneutics distinguishes itself from other modes of thought, such as the explanatory, it presupposes the transcendental difference.

## Apel

Karl-Otto Apel accepts the requirement of the transcendental difference established by Heintel as the condition of hermeneutics and as the final domain of mediation. He calls the domain of the final mediation "the communicative community." The latter encompasses both hermeneutics and the sciences, and indeed is a condition for intercultural understanding. He argues for the primacy of the communicative community along the following lines. 1) The positivistic and neopositivistic schools of language argue either for axiomatically constructed language or for empirically descriptive language. The problem is that both presuppose a broader language for which they cannot account. It is assumed that the speakers maintaining the two distinct linguistic theories are communicating about their positions; such a communication requires a language that is shared by both speakers and which permits their mutual understanding of one another. This language is the assumed hermeneutical understanding and belongs to a tradition of a communicating community. The communicating community and its linguistic understanding is a condition for various specific modes of linguistic constructions and descriptive statements, and, indeed, any objectified mode of theorizing about language. 2) Yet the communicative community, with its linguistic understanding stemming from a historically accumulated speech, is inadequate for cross-cultural communication. After all, different cultures presuppose distinct communicative communities, possessing distinct hermeneutical traditions, i.e., modes of interpreting the world. The very experience of the difference between our own and a foreign mode of interpretation, and the comparison between them, presupposes, according to Apel, a communicative community as a mediating process that is broader than any historically transmitted tradition.[21]

Apel claims that this final point of mediation can be introduced into any tradition and specific situations and indeed it can be applied to the current problems of cross-cultural relationships.[22] What Apel suggests here is what Johannes Lohmann called "pan-linguistics."[23] It is a reflective process

capable of understanding the meanings of its own hermeneutical tradition and the traditions of others. Such an understanding of meanings reveals the limits of one's own linguistic interpretations and those of other cultures. This understanding
is most crucial, according to Apel, in the contemporary encounter of various cultures, specifically with respect to the introduction of Western technology into cultures that are pre-
technological. It is essential to assume a mediating process, a
communicative level, that can make sense of Western scientism
and African tribalism. This is the area toward which Apel di-
rects his theoretical reflections.[24]

The first problem lies in the question of reflection upon a
particular tradition: do reflection and a critique weaken the
tradition? They may become a disruption of a tradition and
result in a distantiation of an individual from the immediacy of
the force of a tradition. The question can be stated in stronger
terms: does the introduction of a radical novelty compel the
inhabitants to reflect upon their tradition and thus disrupt it
radically? Gadamer would say no; after all, the hermeneutical
understanding, as historically effective consciousness, would incorporate the novelty and interpret it in terms of the given
tradition and its linguistic understanding. Yet Apel points out
that, for example, the introduction of massive industrial production and technology disempowered the preindustrial tradition and its modes of understanding and living. This is more
obvious in the disruption of a traditional continuity, of a traditional historically effective consciousness, among the non-
Western cultures.

The traditional cultures that accept the Western technocratic
modalities of understanding and living are compelled to assume a greater distance from their traditions than was the case
in the West. These cultures cannot even conceive of how to
bridge the gap between their historically effective consciousness and the novel and disruptive mode of thought. From the
very outset they are compelled to establish a quasi-scientific
hermeneutics of historical planetary process into which they
are being swept, a process that stems from another hermeneutical tradition which was established without their participation.
By an unavoidable distantiation, by the disruption of their own
historically effective consciousness, they are made aware explicitly of their own moralities, religions, and modes of life.
They are compelled to objectify their own hermeneutical

understanding. In this sense they seek out a reflective process, a hermeneutical-scientific orientation capable of mediating their own tradition and the incoming understanding. This mediating process should illuminate their own traditions and at the same time account for the intrusion of the scientific-technological mode of thought. This is the reason why the quasi-scientific philosophy of Marxism is so attractive to the intellectuals of the third world.[25]

Following these reflections Apel opts for an establishment of complementarity between hermeneutical and scientific-technological thought. Indeed, he opts for their mediation. This mediating process he calls "quasi-scientific."[26] It includes both complementary pairs, explanation and hermeneutics, sciences and humanities. Apel accepts the claim that the hermeneutical understanding of a tradition is more fundamental than any scientific modality within a tradition. Yet the hermeneutical tradition retains an "irrationalism" insofar as it excludes the function of natural forces and material compulsions dealt with by the natural sciences. Yet the understanding of such forces requires a distantiation, requires a "nonparticipatory" observation of natural events. To exemplify the conjunction of hermeneutics and the physical-technological sciences, Apel uses a model drawn from psychology. In a psychiatric situation the hermeneutical understanding of the patient must be deliberately disrupted by the psychiatrist, who not only maintains a dialogue with the patient at the hermeneutical level but also assumes a distance from the patient's self-understanding in order to provide an explanation of the patient's malady. The psychiatrist assumes a mediating reflection between the hermeneutical understanding of the patient and the scientific explanation of the patient's problem. Having provided an explanation, the psychiatrist can lead the patient to integrate the explanation into the patient's hermeneutical understanding and self-interpretation within his/her tradition.[27]

Such a quasi-scientific model should be applied, according to Apel, to the cultures that are being disrupted by Western scientific-technological modes of thought, to the cultures that are becoming historical, i.e., are compelled to reflect upon their own histories and traditions instead of being directly immersed in them. Such cultures can use the explanatory model to understand their economic situation in relationship to the rest of the world, to understand the economic forces functioning as causes in their own social life, and at the same time to interpret the forces in terms of their own hermeneutical understanding. This is not to say that the hermeneutical understanding of their own traditions will remain completely unchanged; rather, now it will include the previously unexplicated "irrational" forces in the form of scientific accounts.

This model leads Apel to assume a point of mediation between social-scientific explanatory procedures and the historical-hermeneutical understanding of the meaning of events. The use of this model would allow the supersession of the irrational moments of a hermeneutical understanding by explanatory procedures and in turn alter the latter by the changed hermeneutical understanding. The latter would remain broader and more encompassing than the scientific-explanatory model. The mediating process becomes a "pan-linguistic" condition or a communicating community capable of correlating the scientific-technological procedures established in one culture and the hermeneutical tradition of another culture. This "communicating community" can no longer belong to any hermeneutical understanding of a particular culture. It is a condition of all human understanding of science and culture. It comprises a mediating process that in its "commonality" is the condition for the understanding of differences.

## Poeggeler

While accepting the critiques of Heintel and Apel of Gadamerian hermeneutics, Otto Poeggeler expands the meaning of hermeneutics to include the scientific-technological explanatory model not as secondary to, but as equal with, the historically effective consciousness. The explanatory sciences are a mode of interpreting the world and play a crucial role in the understanding of human affairs. Hence hermeneutics must be extended by what he calls "mantic phenomenology." By this he means a descriptive account having a predictive capacity. The predictive scientific process is also called by Poeggeler "Pythagoreanism." It provides a mathematical-technical interpretation of natural events and history.[28]

The quest by the sciences to decipher nature mathematically seems to lead to nontemporal and hence nonhistorical understanding. This seems to run counter to the basic hermeneutical orientation. Yet Poeggeler insists that if hermeneutics is to be taken at its fundamental level, then it cannot create an opposition between itself and mantic phenomenology. If hermeneutics deals with the humanities, with what is human, then the sciences are parts of humanities; they constitute human activity. Hermeneutics must include the meaning of the mantic and the humanistic languages. It must raise the question concerning the mantic interpretation of the world and the limits of such an interpretation. Moreover, we can speak of mantic phenomenology as a part of the historically effective consciousness, since such phenomenology was developed in history and has its own horizons and internal limitations. After all, the mantic phenomenology of Newton developed out of pre-Newtonian interpretation of nature. It is sufficient to glance at the literature of that time to become convinced that the controversies, for example between Newton and Leibniz (through their intermediaries), concerning the interpretation of space, time, and movement, were very much a historical-hermeneutical process.[29] The same is true of the interpretations of the basic "stuff" of the universe, a problem so well apparent in the controversy between Locke and Leibniz.[30] Although the Newtonian mantic phenomenology possessed a "seeming eternity," it was challenged and limited by the development of Einsteinian mantic phenomenology. The latter also appeared in the context of a historically developed problem of mantic phenomenology. Thus, Poeggeler claims, it is incorrect to speak of mantic phenomenology as abstract and remote from the world of human understanding and the historically effective consciousness. If one were to oppose hermeneutics to mantic phenomenology, the opposition would be based not on hermeneutics but on a prejudgment of a particular hermeneuticist.

Poeggeler argues against Gadamer's understanding of modern science as being motivated merely by the desire for technological control of nature. Indeed, many hermeneuticists have claimed that the mantic phenomenology became absolutized and dogmatic. They assume that while hermeneutics is concerned with the understanding of specific historical situations with relative and finite validity of linguistic pronouncements, the mantic phenomenology attempts to claim universal validity irrespective of place and time. Yet Poeggeler points out that it is precisely the influence of mantic thought which has led not to absolutization but to relativization of understanding. Such thought, in fact, relativized the concepts of "place, movement, length, above-below," showing that these are not absolute but, rather, constitute invariants only within a very specific set of conditions. Indeed, there may be a vulgarization of mantic thought, claiming calculatability of all events and for all times. Yet this is merely a positivistic metaphysics having nothing to do with mantic phenomenology. No serious thinker in this area would make a claim without first delimiting precise conditions under which the claim could be valid.[31]

Poeggeler contests the interpretation of mantic thought as a means for technological violation of nature. First of all, technological intervention in nature need not be exploitative; it can be discovering. Astronomical instruments aid in the discovery of the composition and the expanse of the universe, the macrocosmos. The electronic microscope aids our understanding of the microcosmos.[32] While the Newtonian mechanistic interpretation is viable, it is only one way of understanding the world, and does not necessarily reduce the human to a mechanistic self-interpretation, unless the human decides to accept such an interpretation. Indeed, it is possible to interpret the universe mechanistically and, retrogressively, to interpret the human in the same way. This is precisely the historically effective consciousness that allows us to interpret ourselves mechanistically. As the Chinese saying goes, Who does his business mechanically, acquires a mechanical heart. Yet Poeggeler insists that technological thought is not a product of modern mantic phenomenology, but has deeper roots in our use of tools and our bodies for the shaping of nature for human needs.[33] We do not interpret science technologically because of our mantic thought, but because for thousands of years humans used any invention to intervene in nature in order to fulfill various needs.

Poeggeler claims that there can and must be a bridge between mantic thought and hermeneutics, specifically if we raise the question concerning the meaning of the physical sciences for the humanities and for historical human life in general. At the same time the repeatability of mantic thought, the reiteration of the conditions under which some events could take place, leads to a stable point of reference from which historical reflections may be possible. History cannot be grasped historically, even if it is modish to attempt such a venture. Although various mantic logics and laws are discovered historically, e.g., the principle of noncontradiction or Newtonian laws, we cannot say that they are valid for particular historical times. Rather, they are valid anytime we wish to think logically or under mechanistic requirements. This does not mean that these discoveries are metaphysical; rather they must be seen as structures that are essentially repeatable despite the vicissitudes of historical understanding. While it is true that the historically effective consciousness is valid, it is also true we can acquire permanent structures that are valid anytime given the required conditions. Of course, the structures may require hermeneutical understanding for their interpretation to the lay population. And that points to the original conception from which hermeneutics derives: *Hermes,* the messenger of gods, who translates divine edicts into humanly comprehensible language. The discoveries of mantic phenomenology may also require such a translation and interpretation through which mantic thought becomes a part of the historically effective consciousness.

The hermeneutical understanding has undergone the transformations described above not as a result of external influences but in its internal self-evaluation. It has emerged in contemporary thought to face the crises of the sciences and the humanities and to confront the question arising from the intercultural disruptions occurring in the various parts of the globe. It is historically true, as Dilthey points out, that hermeneutics made itself felt during the periods of crises and transitions. It was called to interpret novelties in old terms, or to interpret old modes of thought in terms of new understanding. At the same time it was called to explicate and interpret general and "universal" edicts in specific situations and concrete cases. The contemporary emergence of hermeneutical philosophy is an indication that our age is one of transition and requires the aid of hermeneutics.

## Notes

1. Otto Poeggeler, *Hermeneutik und Philosophie* (Munich: Nymphenburger, 1972), p. 10.
2. Ibid., p. 11.
3. Thomas Seebohm, "The Problem of Hermeneutics in Recent Anglo-American Literature, Part 1," in *Philosophy and Rhetoric* 10, no. 3 (1977): 180ff.

64 RHETORIC, LITERATURE, AND INTERPRETATION

4. Martin Heidegger, *Sein und Zeit* (Tübingen: Niemeyer, 1960), pp. 32ff.

5. Hans-Georg Gadamer, *Wahrheit und Methode* (Tübingen: Mohr, 1960), p. 255.

6. Ibid., p. xxi. Translations from Gadamer and other sources cited in this essay are my own.

7. Ibid., pp. 289ff.

8. Ibid., p. xvi.

9. Ibid., pp. 105ff.

10. Ibid., p. 265.

11. Jürgen Habermas, "Zur Gadamers 'Wahrheit und Methode,' " in *Hermeneutik und Ideologiekritik,* ed. Jürgen Habermas (Frankfurt: Suhrkamp, 1971), p. 49.

12. Gadamer, *Wahrheit und Methode,* p. 268.

13. Hans-Georg Gadamer, "Rhetorik, Hermeneutik und Ideologiekritik," in *Hermeneutik und Ideologiekritik,* ed. Habermas, p. 79.

14. Hans-Georg Gadamer, *Vernunft im Zeitalter der Wissenschaft* (Frankfurt: Suhrkamp, 1976), p. 9.

15. Erich Heintel, "Verstehen und Erklären," in *Hermeneutik als Weg heutiger Wissenschaft,* ed. Rudolph Warnach (Salzburg: Anton-Pastet, 1971), p. 68.

16. Ibid., p. 70.

17. Ibid., p. 73.

18. Erich Heintel, *Einführung in die Sprachphilosophie* (Darmstadt: Wissenschaftliche Buchgesellschaft, 1972), pp. 59ff.

19. Ibid., p. 61.

20. Ibid., chap. 3.

21. Karl-Otto Apel, "Die Kommunikationsgemeinschaft als transcendentale Voraussetzung der Sozialwissenschafte," in *Dialog als Methode* (Göttingen: Vandenhoeck & Ruprecht, 1972), pp. 4ff.

22. Karl-Otto Apel, "Szientistik, Hermeneutik, Ideologiekritik," in *Hermeneutik und Ideologiekritik,* ed. Habermas, p. 35.

23. Johannes Lohmann, "Erfahrung und Denken," *Wiener Zeitschrift für Philosophie, Psychologie und Pädagogik* 8, nos. 3–4 (1966): 83ff.

24. Apel, "Szientistik, Hermeneutik, Ideologiekritik," p. 34.

25. Ibid., p. 37.

26. Ibid., p. 43.

27. Ibid., p. 39.

28. Otto Poeggeler, "Hermeneutische und mantische Phänomenologie," *Philosophische Rundschau* 13 (1965): 4.

29. Kurt Lasswitz, *Geschichte der Atomistik vom Mittelalter bis Newton,* vol. 2 (Darmstadt: Wissenschaftliche Buchgesellschaft, 1963).

30. Gottfried-Wilhelm Leibniz, *Nouveaux essais sur l'entendement humaine,* vol. 2 (Frankfurt: Insel Verlag, 1961).

31. Poeggeler, "Hermeneutische und mantische Phänomenologie," p. 11.

32. Ibid., p. 13.

33. Ibid., p. 12.

# Psychomythology:
# The Case of H.D.

## Marylin B. Arthur

Wesleyan University

**P**SYCHOANALYSIS, the disenchanting product of the dis-
enchantment of the world,"[1] struggles still, in spellbound
fascination, against the alluring enticement of the image in the
pool, the self-love of Narcissus, curse of his self-knowledge.
Hence, the self-*re*flexive project of masculine identity—to *re*-
cover oneself as presence. Narcissus: pure exteriority, a dou-
bling of the external, a presence without an absence, a self
without an other. And beside the doubled presence of Narcissus—the doubled absence of Echo. Absence of body—"only her
voice has life," and absence of speech—"she cannot speak first,
she can only imitate what she hears." The self-*de*flexive project
of feminine identity—to *dis*cover oneself as absence. Echo: pure
interiority, dis-embodied voice, an absence without a presence,
an other without a self.[2]

If psychoanalysis sets out to bring to the surface the unconscious of literature, then literature, in its turn, may function as
"the unconscious of psychoanalysis," as Shoshana Felman has
suggested.[3] This is nowhere clearer than in Ovid's tale, which
dramatizes as tragic flaw what psychoanalysis has only recently
discovered as its "error,"[4] its mis-taking of the masculine image
for the human ideal.

In Aristotle "a woman is as it were an infertile male; the
female, in fact, is female on account of inability of a sort." "We
should look upon the female state as being as it were a defor-
mity, though one which occurs in the ordinary course of nature." "Nature has in a way strayed from the generic type. The
first beginning of this deviation is when a female is formed

instead of a male."[5] Psychoanalysis has only just come to know
itself as the father's son of this ancient theoretical discourse—as
the legitimate, patrilineal descendant of the phallocentric paradise of ancient Greece. But there is a paradox here. For if, on
one level, the male body has been given pride of place in
psychoanalytic theory, then on another level the privileged
voice has been that of the female—and precisely the voice that
does not speak, the guardian of the repressed text, the language of the "private theater" (Anna O.),[6] the silences of the
hysteric. If psychoanalysis studies what Lacan calls "lacunary
phenomena,"[7] if it seeks to know "the discourse of the Other,"[8]
to gain access to the shadowy, hidden realm of the interior, the
private world of basic human desires—then historically this has
been the privileged domain of the female.

However, this status as "Other," as referent within what Derrida and others have identified as the logocentric project of
Western metaphysics, renders problematic in its turn the
theoretical status of the woman's discourse.[9] For the dichotomi-
zation of thought that demands such oppositions as rea-
son/passion, culture/nature, active/passive, etc., attracts the
male/female polarity into its orbit, and teratogenizes the female writer. In the act of lifting up the pen she becomes a
monstrous birth, an androgyne, the phallic mother. In short,
she is denaturalized, and the world is turned, not so much
upside down, as inside out.

Few writers have so insistently located themselves within the
center of this psychoanalytic and semiological whirlpool as
H.D., the American expatriate poet known best for her association with the Imagist school that flourished briefly in British
and American literary circles in the second decade of this century. H.D. was analyzed by Freud in 1933 and 1934, and she
wrote an account of this experience called *Tribute to Freud*. It
was to be expected, then, that the earliest extensive critical
treatment of her work should have adopted a psychoanalytic
approach.[10] And it was further to be expected that this critical
exegesis should have taken the form of a reenactment of the
Narcissus and Echo myth, in which the male/critic/analyst
hears the voice of the female/poet/patient as a lamentation
over loss, incompleteness, subjectivity, and insubstantiability.

Susan Friedman, the author of a full-length treatment of
H.D.,[11] has also conducted a brilliant analysis of this instance of

the sexual politics of the production of meaning in literary analysis.[12] But it is not to the "flagrant misogyny"[13] of the interpretive enterprise that I want to call attention at this time. Rather, I want to point to certain ways in which the theoretical impasses to which I alluded earlier have rendered problematic the very enterprise of the psychoanalytic criticism of the text of H.D.

If psychoanalytic theory privileges the opposition between masculine and feminine, then it is also the case that H.D. inscribed that opposition at the center of her poetic vision, and that she exploited it in a manner which is entirely consonant with Freudian doctrine. For, from the time of her earliest writings, H.D., like many other poets and artists of her era, drew consciously not only on the elements of psychoanalytic theory that were being popularized widely in the early part of this century, but on the dream imagery of French Symbolist poetry. In this respect, *Tribute to Freud, Advent, The Gift,* and other explicitly psychobiographical statements seem merely to formulate in a different register the categories, ideas, and themes that permeate the entire corpus of H.D.'s work.

Thus, Joseph Riddel has claimed that "H.D.'s primary myth insists on a Freudian interpretation."[14] The myth to which he refers is, as he formulates it, the isolation and threatened nothingness of the subjective and feminine self, which attempts to project itself outward into the hard, masculine, and objective other. Now such a myth partakes of nothing so much as of the stereotypical components that make up, within Western culture, the opposition between masculine and feminine. And psychoanalytic theory, as is well known, is predicated on nothing so much as these same stereotypes, whose lineaments and whose insistent intrusion into all aspects of thought, life, and culture psychoanalytic theory sets out to bring to light. The Freudian "interpretation," then, on which H.D.'s myth is said to insist, is nothing other than Freudian theory itself—the 1931 essay on "Female Sexuality," say, construed as a master narrative operating beneath the surface of the poetry.[15]

This kind of "interpretation," this "Freudian criticism"— about which it has been remarked that "the only people still seriously interested in it are the Freudians [i.e., Freudian analysts] themselves"[16]—has occasioned, as is well known, a massive crisis of confidence within contemporary critical theory, and the Lacanian rereading of Freud has been called in to heal the breach.[17] The standard epithet hurled at this Freudian criticism is "reductionistic," but I want to argue that it is not so much the "reduction of illusions"[18] that is at issue here as it is the tautological nature of the enterprise. And this, I submit, is most especially evident in a poet like H.D., for whom the themes and language of psychoanalysis constitute what might be called her poetic vocabulary.

Let me cite as an example one critic's claim that H.D.'s idea of the self as a shellfish containing within itself a spell that continuously generates outer coral is an example of a compensatory fantasy.[19] And let me juxtapose to this a statement of H.D.'s that she wrote in 1929 as an answer to a "Confessions-Questionnaire" in *Little Review*. She said:

> I don't think I want to change places with anyone else because surely each one of us is a world to himself, a shell-fish of his own making. "We" are all the same at root, all just one of those protoplasmic germs or spheres or globes that Plato talks about. "We" differentiate one from the other only by the shell and as the shell is MY shell and as I have made this particular shell for my own particular line of defense, I can't see what I should or could want with anybody's shell but my own.[20]

When H.D. identifies the shell-fish fantasy as a defensive gesture, can we claim to have been enlightened by the critic who explains it to us as a compensatory fantasy?

On the other hand, as some of the more ardent neo-Freudians like Karen Horney discovered, the concept of penis envy has a correlate in the sociological realities of patriarchal culture that the concept castration fear does not. Or, to put it in another way, when Plato in the *Menexenus* (238A) claims that "the woman in her conception and generation is but the imitation of the earth, and not the earth of woman," he is drawing attention to the ambiguous status of the female in Western discourse, and to her troubled relationship to the opposition between signifier and signified. In contemporary French feminist literary theory,[21] the question is posed as that of women's "access to culture" within a system in which culture is the masculine privilege and nature belongs to the woman.

For H.D., as feminist critics have pointed out,[22] the oxymoronic quality of the designation "female poet" was both an implicit and explicit concern. H.D. records, primarily in the prose works, her anxiety about her own creative power, and her fears that the male poet would seek to control it, to stifle it, or to relegate her to the status of his muse.[23]

Thus, the second obstacle to a psychoanalytic approach to the poetry of H.D. has to do with what some critics have called the theoretical location of the female authorial "I." That is, does the woman who, as a poet, takes over, as it were, the privileged male domain of the production of meaning, write "for" women, "as" a woman, or as a man? Or does she, as H.D. seems often to have done, locate herself in the ambiguous territory of the boundary between the sexes?

The problems that confront us under the general heading "Psychoanalysis and Gender," then, can be defined with reference to H.D. in two ways. The first has to do with the demystification of psychoanalytic categories themselves, and our need to call them into question as explanatory mechanisms in the case of poets like H.D., who consciously and deliberately draw upon them. The second has to do with certain sociological and cultural realities that automatically define the female writer as a kind of androgyne, and which demand that as a female writer she call into question her own "femininity" and its relationship to "masculinity."

As is well known, psychoanalytic interpretation—narrowly conceived—tends to disregard the latter problem, or to reduce it to its unconscious manifestation as penis envy. There is, however, one poem of H.D.'s that formulates the problem of the female as creative artist in psychosexual terms, and which exploits the opposition between masculine and feminine, male and female. But, as we shall see, in order to read it psychoanalytically, we shall have to abandon any attempts to produce a Freudian "master narrative" of the conjunction of male and female. To be sure, we shall encounter many opportunities for it in this poem, whose title, "Red Roses for Bronze," invites us to unmask the heavy metal and enchanting glitter of the bronze that endures as phallic glory, and to see the passionate blossoms which sift into dust as the ephemeral, insubstantial (nonexistent?) female genitals. But we shall resist these enticements in pursuit of a greater pleasure-gain—that of restoring meaning to the encounter itself. To this extent we shall be seeking to recover (and to uncover) a "sex [that] is defined mythologically [or symbolically], and not biologically."[24]

## Red Roses for Bronze

### I

If I might take a weight of bronze
and sate
my wretched fingers
in ecstatic work,
if I might fashion
eyes and mouth and chin,
if I might take dark bronze
and hammer in
the line beneath your underlip
(the slightly mocking,
slightly cynical smile
you choose to wear)
if I might ease my fingers and my brain
with stroke,
stroke,
stroke,
stroke,
stroke at—something (stone, marble, intent,
    stable, materialized)
peace,
even magic sleep
might come again.

### II

All very well
while all the others smirked,
to turn and smile:
you thought that I might see your joke,
would do
(fault of a better)
for the moment anyhow;
you knew
that I would prove too strange, too proud,
for just the ordinary sort of come and go,
the little half-said thing,
the half-caught smile,
the subtle little sort of differentiating
between the thing that's said
and that's said not;
the "have I seen you somewhere else?
forgot? impossible,"
the half-caught back half-smile,
the interrupted nod,
"a clod
may hold the rarest flower,
so I?"

the question that's an answer
and the thing
that means that what's said
isn't answering;
this,
this,
or this,
or this thing
or the other;
the casual sort of homage that you care
to flick toward this
or this odd passing whim;
the one above the second on the marble stair,
the smaller (or the taller) of those two,
chattering,
chattering
by the fountain-rim.

### III

I count most men ignoble by your height,
neither too tall,
for some taste
none too slight,
but sensing underneath the garment seam
ripple and flash and gleam
of indrawn muscle
and of those more taut,
I feel that I must turn and tear and rip
the fine cloth
from the moulded thigh and hip,
force you to grasp my soul's sincerity,
and single out
me,
me,
something to challenge,
handle differently.

### IV

I'd say,
come let me start the thing at once,
to-day—
to-morrow will not do at all;
I've got a studio
near the Olympieum,
it's cold in winter,
in summer—well
the heat
forbids an adequate comparison;

they say discomfort
prods the ardent soul on;
why must they vent on artists
all their venom?
though that, of course, is all
beside the question—
I mean
come now,
to-day;
forgive me; your dark hair
catches the light
in serpent curves,
here,
there;
that shimmer on the bay-leaf
where the sun
catches the bronze-green glint,
bay-leaf
or palm,
the sort of thing that spreads its ripple on
over across the helmets
to the stars;

you might be Mars
or maybe Actaeon
the Huntress
bids her hounds
to leap upon.

V

I'd hide my fervour in
"that sort of thing,
you know how tiresome it is,"
begin my mastery
in ironic wise,
making of mouth and eyes
a thing of mystery
and invidious lure,
so that all, seeing it, would stare,
so that all men (seeing it)
would forsake all women
(chattering)
I'd make a thing at last,
downright,
not in the least
subtle
or insinuating;

such is my jealousy and such my hate

though I would state it otherwise,
say;
"as a favour,
just that turn of chin,
something I've waited for,
you know the judges at the Pythian games,
the classic note,
the touch the world proclaims
perfection;
tiresome?
but I must finish what I have begun,
the tall god standing
where the race is run";

such is my jealousy
(that I discreetly veil
with just my smile)
that I would clear so fiery a space
that no mere woman's love could long endure;
and I would set your bronze head in its place,
about the base,
my roses would endure,
while others,
those, for instance,
she might proffer,
standing by the stair,
or any tentative offers of white flowers
or others lesser purple at the leaf,
must fall and sift and pale
in (O so short a space)
to ashes and a little heap of dust.

"Red Roses for Bronze," the title poem of a 1931 volume,[25] raises interpretive questions by its very title. Are we to understand that the red roses are offered as a gift for the bronze, or that they are posited as a substitute *for* bronze? The poem, as we shall see, does not resolve this issue, but insists on sustaining the ambiguity.

"Red Roses for Bronze" is composed of five sections of unequal length. In the first section the artist claims, "If I might take a weight of bronze / and sate / my wretched fingers / in ecstatic work . . . peace, / even magic sleep / might come again." This sensual approach to the hard substance ("stone, marble, intent, / stable, materialized") is an approach only, acted out as a coitus interruptus, an artistic gesture experienced as an ecstatic transport deflected immediately into cessation of activity. No consummation of objet d'art is envisioned here, for in its stead there is the harsh deflection into aggression. In the long ellipsis that separates protasis from apodosis in the long sentence which comprises the first section, the artist's impulses are soothed through an attack on the "weight of bronze." For she will "hammer in" her male subject's "slightly mocking, / slightly cynical smile," and she will "ease my fingers and my brain" with a stroking, which she repeats as the verb "stroke" in asyndeton five times, adding to the final occurrence an "at" ("stroke at—"), which converts the soothing gesture into a hostile one.

Thus, for the female artist, the creative impulse, experienced as sexual transport, is automatically linked with a hostility toward the male that is the occasion for appearance of the impulse. At the same time, the threat that the male poses is controlled by transforming him from sexual being into artifact.

The second section of the poem elaborates on the smile of the first strophe, a smile that is now inserted into the social milieu of a party where it takes on the quality of a flirtatious gesture—"the casual sort of homage that you care / to flick toward this / or this odd passing whim." The artist, who locates herself outside of this "ordinary come and go" of the "chattering, / chattering, / by the fountain-rim," imagines a tentative communion of spirits between herself and the man who turns to her and smiles: "you thought that I might see your joke, / would do / (fault of a better) / for the moment anyhow; / you knew / that I would prove too strange, too proud, / for just the ordinary sort of come and go." At the same time, this long section is replete with examples of the gallantry and flirting of men and women, which the artist defines as meaningless, arbitrary, and frivolous gestures that belong to the conventional world of male/female relations.

This section of the poem makes it clear that the woman, as artist, feels herself alienated from the ordinary world of relations between men and women. What is more, she denigrates the women of this world ("chattering, / chattering"), a milieu where, as she sees it, men's interest in women is insincere ("you thought that I . . . would do / (fault of a better) / for the moment anyhow"). Her role as artist, then, also frees her from female vulnerability.

The third section of the poem pivots on a slightly incomplete reversal of the sexes. The artist now pays homage to the man, but it is not the kind of casual homage that his patronizing smiles and nods gave to the chattering women. Rather, she

claims for herself as artist a finer, truer, sensibility, a capacity to
sense "underneath the garment seam" the godlike quality of his
male body, a body which she later compares to that of an Olym-
pic victor. At the same time, if she tears "the fine cloth / from
the moulded thigh and hip," by this gesture he will recognize
her "soul's sincerity," will single her out as "something to challenge, / handle differently."

In the fourth section of the poem, the artist effects an important strategic move. With the exception of the last five lines,
which I shall treat separately, the entire section is taken up with
an imagined flirtation which duplicates that of the second section. Only here the subject of conversation is the small and
trifling difficulties that beset the artist:

> I'd say
> come let me start the thing at once,
> to-day—
> to-morrow will not do at all;
> I've got a studio
> near the Olympieum,
> it's cold in winter,
> in summer—well
> the heat
> forbids an adequate comparison;
> they say discomfort
> prods the ardent soul on;
> why must they vent on artists
> all their venom?
> though that, of course, is all
> beside the question—

As artist, then, the woman can openly solicit male attention.
She can act as temptress, seductress; she can play on the narcis-
sistic male ego in a manner that she cannot or will not do as
"mere" woman. As artist, she takes the active role in a sublimated form of sexual intercourse—she undresses him, she
expects him to recognize in this act the sign of her heated
passion.

In the last five lines of this section the artist compares her
subject to Mars, and then to the "Actaeon / the Huntress / bids
her hounds / to leap upon." The myth to which H.D. alludes is a
revealing one: when the hunter Actaeon encountered the virgin goddess Artemis bathing nude, the goddess interpreted the
act as a violation, and in retaliation for Actaeon's crime threw a
deerskin over him so that his own hounds leapt upon him and

destroyed him. Thus, although the artist flirts with the male, flatters him, she also polarizes him as Mars/Actaeon—Mars the lover of Venus, Actaeon destroyed by Artemis. And she also polarizes herself—whore or virgin.

In the fifth and final section of the poem, the artist admits her sexual passion, and acknowledges her flirtatious and flattering gestures as tokens meant to hide her "fervour," her "jealousy," and her "hate." The sculpting itself is an act of irony and of mastery, for she will fashion a statue that will be "an invidious lure," an irresistible attraction for both men and women.

In the last part of the last section, the artist returns to the themes of the poem's first section. Now it is her smile that parenthetically intrudes as she prepares to "clear [a] fiery . . . space" with which no "mere woman's love" could compete. This abstract sexualization of the artistic field into which the head and base of the statue are collapsed concludes with a disparagement of a nameless other woman's "white flowers / or others less purple at the leaf"—a displacement, perhaps, of the proud, angry virgin of the poem's first section, here recovered as rival. And now the coitus interruptus of the earlier section is completed, in a flourish with which the female takes possession of the male.

In the elaborate gesture with which the poem concludes, the artist has taken on the role of Pygmalion, and she has transposed the roles of male and female—she is the artist, the creator, the active one; he is the artifact, the created, the passive adored and static other, imprisoned in bronze, voiceless, and with a hollow interior.

"Red Roses for Bronze" gives us, then, as the barely veiled terms of its poetic discourse, an opposition between the sexes conceived in its most stereotypical form. But into this sexually charged field—which only continues to exist as such to the extent that we resist a stark unmasking of its starkly sexual symbols—there intrudes an artistic project cast in the language of flirtation between the sexes. The artistic project is thus libidinized, and the artistic gesture—the embrace both passionate and hostile—wavers tentatively between a sublimated and a fully sexualized form.

We could, to be sure, read this poem in such a way as to uncover its "illusions"—to see in the language and themes of the artistic project a gesture of "bad faith," an example of a

repressed sexuality whose aims and ambitions refuse open ac-
knowledgment. I have not chosen this avenue of approach.
Instead, I have attempted a psychoanalytic reading that hovers,
along with the poem which is its subject, on the edge of explicit
articulation of the explicitly sexual symbols of the poem. To put
it in the terms which Paul Ricoeur offers,[26] I have chosen "interpretation conceived as the recollection or restoration of
meaning" over "interpretation conceived as the unmasking,
demystification, or reduction of illusions."[27]

## Notes

1. Pierre Bourdieu, *Outline of a Theory of Practice*, trans. Richard Nice (Cambridge:
Cambridge University Press, 1977), p. 92. Bourdieu thus characterizes psychoanalysis
in the course of arguing against the heuristic primacy of the biologically defined prop-
erties of the two sexes. And in an important modification of the psychoanalytic point of
view, he specifies further (*Esquisse d'une théorie de la pratique* [Geneva: Droz, 1972]):

> The child's originary relation to the father or mother, or in other words, to the
> paternal and maternal body—a relation which offers the most dramatic opportunity
> for experiencing all of the fundamental oppositions of mythopoetic practice, symbol-
> ically embodied in the opposition between the penis and the vagina—[does not occur
> as the operative principle in the task of constructing the ego, the world, and all
> heterosexual and homosexual relations], except insofar as this relation is a relation
> with objects whose sex is defined mythologically [or symbolically], and not biologi-
> cally. [P. 195, my translation.]

I shall have occasion to return to this formulation when discussing the necessity for not
taking literally, as it were, the vocabulary of psychoanalytic practice, or, to put it
another way, for refusing to "de-code" symbols into the body parts to which they may
be understood to refer.

2. Reference and citations from Ovid, *Metamorphoses* 3.348, 397ff., 358, 368–69.

3. Shoshana Felman, "To Open the Question," *Literature and Psychoanalysis. The Question of Reading: Otherwise*, ed. Shoshana Felman (*Yale French Studies* 55/56 [1977]), p. 10.

4. See Stanley Leavy, *The Psychoanalytic Dialogue* (New Haven, Conn.: Yale University
Press, 1980), p. 66. Psychoanalysis has been taken to task on this question by many; it
should be clear, however, that we are concerned here not with castigation but with such
methodological implications as might derive from this radical decentering of Freudian
theory.

5. Citations from Aristotle, *Generation of Animals*, trans. A. L. Peak, Loeb Classical
Library (Cambridge, Mass.: Harvard University Press, 1943), pp. 103, 461, 401
(728a18, 775a15, 767b7).

6. Breuer refers to Anna O.'s "habit of day-dreaming" as "her 'private theatre.'" In
Josef Breuer and Sigmund Freud, *Studies on Hysteria*, Standard Edition, Vol. 2, ed. and
trans. James Strachey (London: The Hogarth Press and The Institute of Psycho-
Analysis, 1955), p. 41. And Freud himself had frequent recourse in his early works to
the theatrical metaphor in discussing the unconscious, which he, borrowing the idea
from Fechner, called "ein anderer Schauplatz [another scene]." See, e.g., *The Interpreta-*

*tion of Dreams,* Standard Edition, Vols. 4–5, ed. and trans. James Strachey (London: The Hogarth Press and The Institute of Psycho-Analysis, 1953), pp. 48, 536. See also the discussion of Freud's 1905–1906 essay, "Psychopathic Characters on Stage," by Philippe Lacoue-Labarthe, "Theatrum Analyticum," *Glyph* 2 (1977): 122–43, who cites Lyotard's remark on "the privileged status of the theater in Freudian thought and practice, with respect to the other arts" (p. 124).

7. The phrase is hypothetically attributed to Lacan by Stanley Leavy: "[D]reams, jokes, parapraxes and slips, and neurotic symptoms . . . are [Freud's] discoveries of what Lacan . . . would call 'lacunary phenomena,' evidences of unspoken declarations to be read between the lines of manifest statements and actions. They open pathways to an unconscious discourse for which the speaker seeks utterance with the analyst's help." In "The Significance of Jacques Lacan," *Psychoanalytic Quarterly* 46 (1977): 202. Lacan himself, in the essay "Sexuality in the Defiles of the Signifier," speaks of "the reality of the unconscious—that the unconscious is not an ambiguity of acts, future knowledge that is already known not to be known, but lacuna, cut, rupture inscribed in a certain lack." In *The Four Fundamental Concepts of Psycho-Analysis,* ed. Jacques-Alain Miller, trans. Alan Sheridan (London: The Hogarth Press and The Institute of Psycho-Analysis, 1977), p. 153.

8. Lacan's statement, "The unconscious is the discourse of the Other," is well known and appears scattered throughout his writings, e.g., *Écrits. A Selection,* trans. Alan Sheridan (New York: W. W. Norton, 1977), pp. 55, 193, and *The Four Fundamental Concepts of Psycho-Analysis,* p. 133.

9. See the discussion of Mary Jacobus, "The Difference of View," in *Women Writing and Writing About Women,* ed. Mary Jacobus (London: Croom Helm, 1979), pp. 10–21.

10. Joseph N. Riddel, "H.D. and the Poetics of 'Spiritual Realism,'" *Contemporary Literature* 10 (1969): 447–73, and Norman N. Holland, "H.D. and the 'Blameless Physician,'" ibid., pp. 474–506.

11. Susan Friedman, *Psyche Reborn: The Emergence of H.D.* (Bloomington: Indiana University Press, 1981).

12. Susan Friedman, "Who Buried H.D.? A Poet, Her Critics, and Her Place in the 'Literary Tradition,'" *College English* 36 (1975): 801–14.

13. I borrow this colorful phrase from Shoshana Felman, "Women and Madness: The Critical Phallacy," *Diacritics* 5 (1975): 6.

14. Riddel, "H.D. and 'Spiritual Realism,'" p. 448.

15. Or the *Three Essays on the Theory of Sexuality* (1905–1924), with its 1924 postscript "The Infantile Genital Organization of the Libido: A Supplement to the Theory of Sexuality," taken together with subsequent essays like "The Dissolution of the Oedipus Complex" (1924), "Some Psychological Consequences of the Anatomical Distinction Between the Sexes" (1925)—or all of these writings taken together as "the Freudian theory of female sexuality."

16. Fredric Jameson, *The Political Unconscious: Narrative as a Socially Symbolic Act* (Ithaca, N.Y.: Cornell University Press, 1981), p. 65.

17. See, e.g., Shoshana Felman, "Turning the Screw of Interpretation," *Literature and Psychoanalysis,* pp. 94–207.

18. Paul Ricoeur, *Freud and Philosophy: An Essay on Interpretation,* trans. Denis Savage (New Haven, Conn.: Yale University Press, 1970), p. 9.

19. Norman N. Holland, *Poems in Persons: An Introduction to the Psychoanalysis of Literature* (New York: W. W. Norton, 1973).

20. *Little Review* 12 (1929): 364–65.

21. See the anthology *New French Feminisms*, ed. Elaine Marks and Isabelle Courtivron (Amherst, Mass.: University of Massachusetts Press, 1980).

22. See, especially, Rachel Blau DuPlessis, "Family, Sexes, Psyche: an essay on H.D. and the muse of the woman writer," *Montemora* 6 (1979): 137–56.

23. This is articulated as an explicit concern in *End to Torment* (New York: New Directions, 1979) with reference to Ezra Pound. In that work, she speaks of waiting for letters "with the intense apprehension with which I waited almost 50 years ago, when Ezra left finally for Europe. Through the years, I have imposed or superimposed this apprehension on other people, other letters. A sort of *rigor mortis* drove me onward. No, my poetry was not dead but it was built on or around the crater of an extinct volcano. Not *rigor mortis*. No, No! The vines grow more abundantly on those volcanic slopes. Ezra would have destroyed me and the center they call "Air and Crystal" of my poetry" (p. 35).

Different anxieties are aroused by D. H. Lawrence, depicted as Rico in *Bid Me to Live*. See Rachel Blau DuPlessis, "Romantic Thralldom in H.D.," *Contemporary Literature* 20 (1979): 178–203.

24. Bourdieu, *Esquisse*, p. 195 (my translation).

25. H.D. [Hilda Doolittle], *Red Roses for Bronze* (London: Chatto & Windus, 1931).

26. Ricoeur, *Freud and Philosophy*, p. 9.

27. An earlier version of this paper was presented at a panel on "Psychoanalysis and Gender: Some Feminist Approaches" at the Modern Language Association meeting in Houston, Texas, December 1980.

# Murther: The Hypocritic and the Poet

## David Willbern

### State University of New York, Buffalo

> Tu le connais, lecteur, ce monstre délicat,
> —Hypocrite lecteur—mon semblable—mon frère!
> > Baudelaire, "Au lecteur,"
> > *Les Fleurs du mal*

**Y**ES, I know this reader *(c'est moi même)*, and my question is, what sort of literary critic does he make? In answer, I've derived what I might call the art of hypocriticism. That is the practice of getting a poem under my skin, like a hypodermic injection which magically transforms me into a likeness of the poet: a *monstre délicat,* a double who lies somewhere between a perfect clone and Mr. Hyde. I become a temporary *semblable,* or facsimile: "making like" the poem as I read it, re-presenting its words in my own style, pretending that my voice resembles, re-assembles, the voice of the poem. As I read the poet's written words in my own speech, and feel the poet's recorded emotions through my own feelings, I become a reader simulating an other: that is, a hypocrite. Yet not solely a usurper or dissembler. The Greek *hypokrites* was an actor, but more specifically he was an answerer, that other reciprocal voice which created dialogue, turning ritual monologue into drama, providing verbal support for the continuation and development of a mimetic relationship between two personae. Hypocriticism thus underlies its poetic other, simultaneously taking in the poem as it takes it over in imitation. It offers an equal, answering voice— or an equivocation. It is both duplication and duplicity.[1]

At bottom, any criticism involves an interplay of repre-

sentation and resemblance which may enact a primary ambivalence of psychological identification. Becoming like an other
effects a *liking* in both transitive and intransitive modes. It seeks
an affectionate imitation whose embrace also attempts to erase
difference, to assume the identity of the other. At its extreme it
can become an act of incorporation, or usurpation, or reposses-
sion, whereby the original owner (the poet) somehow vanishes,
or is banished, or disowned: a kind of critical homicide which
pretends to read words while erasing their origin—like study-
ing tracks without asking where they came from, or believing
that an echo has no source but its repetitions, only re-sounding.
(For instance, a frequent motive in critical theories insists on
removing the poet from considerations of his poem, so that
only critic and text remain: one on one, the hunter with his
quarry, playing the big game.)

Poet and critic may indeed be rivals—but not solely as an-
tagonists, facing each other across the infinitely thin boundary
of the page whose threshold is the poem, competing for recognition as Author or Authority. They are rivals as well in Shakespeare's sense: "rivals of the watch," like Elsinore's guards
(*Hamlet* 1. 1. 13). That is, they are associates, partners, two who
share a common action. Originally, "rivals" were people who
lived along the same river (Latin *rivalis*), sharing a common
stream which was a source of connection and, as with any
shared boundary, a source of dispute as well. Poet and critic
may seem to be on opposite shores of the text that flows between them, yet they drink from the same stream.

A criticism which only enforces their separation in fact *rives*
them, rending them apart along the thin fissure of the textual
boundary, widening the rift. To cojoin them, as the hypocritic
would wish, is to let opposition flow into association, like a river.
So that the two faces facing each other across the stream become like mirror-images—or even closer: an interface of poet
and critic. Antagonism and separation describe only the discerning qualities of criticism (from Latin *cerno:* divide, distinguish, judge; related to Greek *krinein, kritikos*). Hypocriticism
blurs distinction, offering both poet and critic a role to share—
each breaking bread in a momentary communion of emotion
and thought, a potentially nourishing reciprocity.

The discerning critic is the reader who knows well one
definition of "lector" (Latin, *lego, legere*): to collect, pick out,
peruse, read. He is the hypercritic, the picky reader. But the

verb has another meaning, equally important. *Lego, legare:* to send a representative or legate; to bequeath (as a legacy). This bequest is the poet's gift, and the critic is his beneficiary. (Critics are both poets' legatees and their legates, their representatives. Poems are bequeathed from poets to critics as a legacy, an inheritance preserved as tradition and scrutinized for meaning or appreciated for value: from bequest to inquest.) Hypocriticism ideally combines both kinds of lector: the reader as *hypocrite lecteur,* both assumptive pretender ("I am the other") and answering supporter ("I am the other's co-respondent"). Reading thus becomes an act of resemblance and dissemblance. "Mon semblable"—the French connotes "fellowman" as well as "lookalike"—"mon frère." Poet and critic become brothers in fellowship and in fraternal rivalry. They come to resemble each other, perhaps—like twins, who, in seeking to look more like themselves, succeed in looking more like each other ("un vrai *monstre délicat*").

My own hypocriticism, an instance of which I want to describe, is similarly a delicate de-monstration of the interface I imagine between myself and a poet. It is a picture of two-facedness—but is the appropriate myth that of Janus or Narcissus? Whichever, or both, what follows is one critic's answering voice to one poet's words. My own "answering style"[2] is not poetic (I am nothing if not critical), but inscribes a hypocriticism which combines close reading techniques, psychoanalytic theory, biographical information and inference, personal memories, verbal associations: a host of strategies, some clear, some indistinct, which enable me to see through the poem in at least two senses, as though I see through it to its core (the critic's hubris), while acknowledging that what I'm seeing through are the lenses of the poem, with my own eyes. The poet Robert Duncan once asked, thinking of Freud: "What was it that the feeling and thought in a poem, rising as it did out of a hidden resource, was true to?"[3] I find that secret source within my own reading, in my own thoughts and feelings, as well as in the thoughts and feelings recorded in the poem by the poet. To follow Duncan's hidden metaphor, the river's source derives paradoxically from my own mouth, as I read. Hypocriticism is *derivative.*

But the only way (if at all) to clarify these confusions is to let the poem have its say and then to answer it (both as question and as call). If you will, then, read the poem,[4] I will then play the hypocritic.

## My Mother Would Be a Falconress

My mother would be a falconress,
And I, her gay falcon treading her wrist,
would fly to bring back
from the blue of the sky to her, bleeding, a prize,
where I dream in my little hood with many bells
jangling when I'd turn my head.

My mother would be a falconress,
and she sends me as far as her will goes.
She lets me ride to the end of her curb
where I fall back in anguish.                                  10
I dread that she will cast me away,
for I fall, I mis-take, I fail in her mission.

She would bring down the little birds,
And I would bring down the little birds.
When will she let me bring down the little birds,
pierced from their flight with their necks broken,
their heads like flowers limp from the stem?

I tread my mother's wrist and would draw blood.
Behind the little hood my eyes are hooded.
I have gone back into my hooded silence,                       20
talking to myself and dropping off to sleep.

For she has muffled my dreams in the hood she has made me,
sewn round with bells, jangling when I move.
She rides with her little falcon upon her wrist.
She uses a barb that brings me to cower.
She sends me abroad to try my wings
and I come back to her. I would bring down
the little birds to her
I may not tear into, I must bring back perfectly.
I tear at her wrist with my beak to draw blood,               30
and her eye holds me, anguisht, terrifying.
She draws a limit to my flight.
Never beyond my sight, she says.
She trains me to fetch and to limit myself in fetching.
She rewards me with meat for my dinner.
But I must never eat what she sends me to bring her.

Yet it would have been beautiful, if she would have carried
     me,
always, in a little hood with the bells ringing,
at her wrist, and her riding
to the great falcon hunt, and me                               40
flying up to the curb of my heart from her heart
to bring down the skylark from the blue to her feet,
straining, and then released for the flight.

My mother would be a falconress,
and I her gerfalcon, raised at her will,
from her wrist sent flying, as if I were her own
pride, as if her pride
knew no limits, as if her mind
sought in me flight beyond the horizon.

Ah, but high, high in the air I flew.                        50
And far, far beyond the curb of her will,
were the blue hills where the falcons nest.
And then I saw west to the dying sun—
it seemd my human soul went down in flames.

I tore at her wrist, at the hold she had for me,
until the blood ran hot and I heard her cry out,
far, far beyond the curb of her will  ·

to horizons of stars beyond the ringing hills of the world
    where the falcons nest
I saw, and I tore at her wrist with my savage beak.        60
I flew, as if sight flew from the anguish in her eye beyond her
    sight,
sent from my striking loose, from the cruel strike at her wrist,
striking out from the blood to be free of her.

My mother would be a falconress,
and even now, years after this,
when the wounds I left her had surely heald,
and the woman is dead,                             70
her fierce eyes closed, and if her heart
were broken, it is stilld  ·

I would be a falcon and go free.
I tread her wrist and wear the hood,
talking to myself, and would draw blood.

    As I begin reading the poem, my first responses are pleasurable. I imagine the joy of being a falcon, flying in perfect harmony with a mother's wishes. Then, as I read further, this imagined happiness suddenly withers, metamorphosing into a clinging fear of being abandoned or of failing in some crucial task. I sense the constraint of being muffled, stifled, held in check by hood and hand; I want to break out of this claustrophobia. My speaking voice, as I read aloud, gains energy and excitement around line fifty, and from here on the poem becomes stronger, more vivid, more engaged in risk. Where before Duncan's incantatory repetitions had almost lulled me, now the stresses (my stresses) become angry and desperate: for instance, the "striking . . . strike . . . striking" echo of lines 62–63. Suddenly I understand that to strike out on one's own is an act of aggression against one's own. Leaving home can be violence. Growing up is murder. I remember, when I was about fourteen, my mother confronting me in her bedroom with some now-forgotten act of defiance. She told me she was going to slap me. To stop her I seized both her wrists and held on, hard. She had severe arthritis, and I hurt her. That look of pain and surprise and recognition on her face stays with me now as I recollect that moment. Our eyes meet in something not shared before: "her eye holds me, anguisht, terrifying." I know why Duncan chose those ambiguous adjectives. Her eye is both anguished and terrifying, just as I am at that moment. Other memories of wounds inflicted by inattention, buried resentment, now surge upon me; anger remains, but just as strongly there is regret. So that the poet's return to captivity at the end of his poem becomes for me a shared act of reparation, as well as an admission of the inability ever really to escape my source, of the eventual impotence of any violent assertion of absolute autonomy. Growing up is first a growing away, high and far, and then a coming back, sometimes too late. Real origins die, and we are left with the re-source of memory, the re-membered images that we carry inside, and which design the shapes of our lives.

A similar notion of the persistent presence of the past seems to have been in Duncan's mind when he wrote of his poetic art:

> Every particular is an immediate happening of meaning at large; every present activity in the poem redistributes future as well as past events. This is a presence extended in a time we create as we keep words in mind.
>
> The immediate event—the phrase within its line, the adjoining pulse in silence, the new phrase—each part is a thing in itself; the junctures not binding but freeing the elements of configuration so that they participate in more than one figure. . . . [The poet] strives not for a disintegration of syntax but for a complication of syntax, overlapping structures, so that words are freed, having bounds out of bound. [*Bow*, p. 1x]

Duncan's remarks about memory and syntax, and the ways in which they look forward and backward while constituting a present moment or structure, are analogous to my own Janus-like notions of the interface of critic and poet, each part of a developing event, paradoxically freed by their conjuncture into a range of flexible and overlapping participations. Reading "My Mother Would Be a Falconress" evokes in me a memory of a moment of adolescent rebellion, and the memory coexists with other, more "literary" responses to the poem. Let me now shift the focus away from private crisis and toward criticism: away from my remembered past to some observations about Duncan's text, in terms of the syntactic complications which he claims give words "bounds out of bound." I find several such syntactic events in "My Mother Would Be a Falconress." The first is in lines 2–4:

> And I . . .
> would fly to bring back
> . . . to her, bleeding, a prize. . . .

Here the ambiguous syntax frees the adjective, "bleeding," to participate in the overlapping figures of falcon, falconress, and prize. One more example, from lines 27–29:

> I would bring down
> the little birds to her
> I may not tear into. . . .

Here the verb, "tear," refers both to the birds and to the falconress, and this dual sense is reinforced by the next line: "I tear at her wrist with my beak to draw blood."

For me, the overall effect of such ambiguous syntactic structures is to blur the boundaries between agents, resulting in a gradually emerging pattern of confusions and shared identities. Such syntax reenforces the tension between unity and separation, fusion and escape, which energizes the drama of the poem. More significantly, the implicit content of these lines describes the developing aggression toward the mother-falconress, which culminates in the repetitive "striking loose" and "striking out" of lines 62–63. Independence, self-liberation, are enacted as assault. Striking out on one's own becomes a blow against family. For Duncan himself, however, this theme may bear more personal power than my own generalization that growing up can be murder. For him, liberation *was* a kind of murder. I suppose that the latent image of a torn and bleeding and finally dead mother which suffuses the poem must evoke for him a very specific event.

The gist of the story I've known perhaps among the first stories I heard, that she died when I was born. Did they say it was in childbirth, because my head was too big, tearing my way through her agony to life? [*Roots,* p. 13]

When I was born, what gave birth to me fell back dead or died in the labor toward my success. Was she alive or dead when I drew my first "breath" and utterd, threw out, my first cry? In taking heart, another heart was lost. What blessing, what key then? [*Roots,* p. 74]

This poet's primal myth, as I read it, is of mother-murder: murther.

Behind his art Duncan identifies at least four mothers. First there is his actual mother who died at his birth in 1919. Then his foster mother who raised him from infancy—except for his first six months when he was "motherless, . . . in the cold" (*Roots,* p. 74)—and who died in 1960, four years before he composed his poem of the falconress. ("After my [foster] mother's death in December 1960," wrote Duncan, "there were two returns of her presence in February and March of 1961. The first came in a dream" [*Roots,* p. 73].) Next there is the poet H.D., his "Mother of mouthings" (*Roots,* p. 86), about whom Duncan has been writing a major book; she died in 1961. Finally there is the mother/*muthos*/muse of his poetry: "'the Mother,'" who, he wrote, "is back of my mothers" (*Roots,* p. 74).

"Mother" is for Duncan (for me, for all of us) an immensely rich word. I've located the following etymological and aural associations in several of his works. (These are my own associations, also found in Duncan's texts.)

MOTHER  *MUTHOS (MYTHOS)* μύζω μυμῦ[5]

MURMUR  MURMURER  DEMURRER

MURTHER  MOUTH  MOUTHINGS  MUTTER

MATTER  METER  MUTE  MUSE

MNEMOSYNE  MEMORY  MAMMARY  MYSTERY

and "Story, Herself a mother of sorts" (*Bow,* p. 67). As I read Duncan, his primary myth, the *muthos*, originates from his idea and experience of the maternal. When he writes, when he remembers, he returns to that original matrix. When I read him, he takes me back along the same psychological and emotional path.

> Mnemosyne, they named her, the
> Mother with the whispering
> featherd wings. Memory,
> the great speckled bird who broods over the
> nest of souls, and her egg,
> the dream in which all things are living,
> I return to, leaving my self.
>
> [*Bow*, p. 10]

Duncan locates the genesis of his "Falconress" poem in dream, when he awoke one morning in 1964 as Saturn, his birth planet, "was brilliant in the early morning sky." The lines, "My mother would be a falconress / and I a falcon at her wrist," kept repeating in his mind. "Was the word *falconress* or *falconess*?" he wondered. "The troubled insistence of the lines would not let go of me." His thoughts led to a memory of "horrible cannibalistic hens, furious in their pecking order" (*Bow*, p. 51). Here, at the poem's dreamlike origin, I sense again a primary confusion of mother and child, falconress and falconess, and the fury of the poet's cannibalistic attack with his own savage beak.[6]

My reading of the seventh stanza of the poem, as a regressive fantasy of harmonious union with the mother-falconress in a state of perfect reciprocity, may then have a uniquely private meaning for Duncan (or, its general human meaning may have uniquely special force). "Yet it would have been beautiful," he writes, "if she would have carried / me always, in a little hood" (ll. 37–38). That is, if he had never been born, but carried always within her womb, in that primal child-hood, his mother would not have been killed by his birth ("tearing [his] way through her agony to life"). I even sense in some of the lines (41–43) the peristaltic rhythms of birth: "straining, and then released for the flight" is to be born, liberated, made separate and free—and also to kill the origin of that liberation.[7] Here, I believe, lie the sources of that primary tension between achievement and loss which I feel in reading Duncan's poetry.

The poet's ambivalent relation to his falconress enacts a drama of the relation of his poetry to his mother tongue. He believes, as I do, that a poet is to his language as a child is to his parents. Duncan's family was deeply interested in esoteric and occult mythologies: theosophy, spiritualism, the Hermetic

Brotherhood, Edenic and Atlantean myth, mystic Neoplaton-
ism (see *Truth*, pp. 8–14). His theory of poetic inspiration is
explicitly a theory of possession, echoing his metaphor of the
"falconress" lines ("the troubled insistence . . . would not let go
of me"):

> The mythic content comes to us, commanding the design of the
> poem; it calls the poet into action, and with whatever lore and craft
> he has prepared himself for that call, he must answer to give body
> in the poem to the formative will. [*Truth*, p. 21]

The muse of this commanding inspiration is maternal: mother
is the *muthos*. "My first mother," he writes, "in whom I took my
first nature, the formal imperative of my physical body and
signature, died when I was born" (*Roots*, p. 74). Duncan's
metaphor suggests his mother as a poetic maker, and himself as
the poem she makes ("formal imperative . . . and signature").
Her felt presence replaces her actual absence. Suffusing the
"silence of concentration" in which he works is the sound of his
mother's voice "singing or crooning" (*Truth*, p. 44). Whenever
he writes, he hears, like the falcon within its hood, the echoing
bells of his childhood, the murmuring *muthos:* "a ringing of
sound in the childhood of the poet's head" (*Bow*, p. 51).

Duncan and I myself, as poet and reader, are ambivalent
about the powers of the falcon's hood. It is comforting and
protective, allowing us to sleep and to dream, but it is also
limiting and claustrophobic, muffling wishes and inhibiting
movement. It is both enabling and disabling, a release (into
dream) and an obsession (of memory). The maternal matrix
animates and delimits the form of poem and of child: it is
simultaneously liberating and controlling. Freed into the
dream of poetry, we are still commanded by the *muthos*.

> She trains me to fetch and to limit myself in fetching.
> She rewards me with meat for my dinner.
> But I must never eat what she sends me to bring her.
>                                                     [Ll. 34–36]

Such a rhythm of permission and inhibition, release and restraint, is a basic structure within my reading of Duncan's
poem. Food becomes a reward for self-deprivation, discipline,
the surrender to form. The formal demands of the mythic
matrix enforce a stark tension in the poem, and on the other
side of filial obedience lies that savage, enraged, cannibalistic

tearing at the mother's body, to draw blood. Duncan's evocation of this elemental ambivalence is, for me, a remarkable achievement, which enables me to recall and feelingly imagine my own private tensions between obedience and rebellion.

This tension is emotional and psychological. I can locate its analogies in my memories, Duncan's biography, ambiguities of syntax within the text, and even in a single word: the term "treading" (lines 3, 18, 70) manages a similar tense complexity. It calls up barnyard images of avian copulation, as well as an aggressive corollary of careful, rhythmic attack, talon by talon. These connotations of sexuality and violence merge with gentler notions of following a path, or of formal, dancelike motion (treading a measure). Duncan's word suggests to me a patterned, obsessive ritual of sexuality and aggression, controlled by a tense obedience to formal command. His vocabulary, like his syntax, and the poem as a whole, unites wish and defense, protecting him as writer and me as reader from the potential dangers it invokes. It is a valuable achievement, and a constant struggle. His poetry, as he says, represents a continual effort to control what he is controlled by, or to shape what is shaping him.

> In the world of saying and telling in which I first came into words, there is a primary trouble, a panic that can still come upon me where the word no longer protects, transforming the threat of an overwhelming knowledge into the power of an imagined reality, or abstracting from a shaking experience the terms for rationalization, but exposes me the more. [*Truth,* pp. 13–14]

> It has seemed to me that I wrestle with the syntax of the world of my experience to bring forward into the Day the twisted syntax of my human language that will be changed in that contest even with what I dread there. And recently I have come to think of Poetry more and more as a wrestling with Form to liberate Form. The figure of Jacob returns again and again to my thought. [*Truth,* pp. 15–16]

This primary panic may be Duncan's response to what lies on the other side of formal poetic utterance: that infantile rage which tears with savage beak—and which dreads the retaliation that might leave it torn and twisted. In its success, breaking through or out of the maternal matrix, it finds fatal isolation. Once free, separate, born, the poet-falcon discovers an image of himself falling and dying:

And then I saw west to the dying sun [son]—
it seemd my human soul went down in flames.

[Ll. 53–54]

Like the mythic Phaeton or Icarus, "the boy Horus, hawk-ghost of the sun" (*Roots,* p. 67), "that hawk, the genius of Poetry" (*Truth,* p. 58), may find his liberation to be his ruin. The myth of Icarus and its analogues is one of Duncan's favorites, along with the stories of Osiris and Orpheus, myths of the poet.

We are<br>
ourselves tears and gestures of Isis<br>
as she searches for what we are ourselves,

Osiris-Kadmon into many men shatterd,
     torn by passion.   She-That-Is,
our Mother, revives ever   His legend.
     She remembers.   She puts it all together.

[*Roots,* pp. 68–69]

The ultimate re-union which Duncan's poetry momentarily establishes for me is its coalescence of two symmetrical and reciprocal images: one of actual physical birth, and the other of the genesis of the word. Our primal bodily origin is "the life-door," "the lips before speech, . . . life's / labia" (*Bow,* pp. 19, 24). Its mimesis is the mouth utterance, spoken *muthos:* the *infans* made into the formal word.

This way below is the way above,
the mouth of the cave or temple growing moist
    shining,   to allow   the neophyte
        full entrance.
The body of the poem, aroused,   having
                what mouths?

[*Bow,* p. 19]

In the poem from which I have taken the above lines ("The Collage"), and in another "(As in the Old Days")," Duncan directly envisions and encounters the bodily image of the matrix: "her cunt   a wound now / the gash in His side" (*Bow,* p. 24). Here the poet re-animates a standard psychoanalytic idea, of the threat which the perception of absence or injury represented by female genitals presents to the male homosexual—the "gay falcon"—who may be disturbed by castration anxiety. My own psychoanalytic perspective constructs a magical, apotropaic fantasy of an undifferentiated, pre-oedipal, "phallic mother"—or of the son-poet-falcon as his mother's magic phallus ("raised at her will")—which underlies the poem, and which may answer to the castration fear. Yet the danger remains. The basic rhythm of extension versus falling, the "dread" of being "cast away," the "dropping off" to sleep, the little birds with broken necks "like flowers limp from the stem," even "the twisted syntax of . . . human language" that Duncan writes of in *Truth,* all suggest to me a fear of catastrophic loss which can be psychoanalytically schematized as castration anxiety.[8]

Yet along with the anxiety is achievement. Duncan's falcon ultimately becomes an image of the poet-child himself and of the poem itself, just as the falconress is an image of his mother(s) and his mythic matrix. Ultimately he enacts her will in him through his poetry: his words are the flights of her will. As he writes of H.D., "his "Mother of mouthings"":

> The lady in the shade of the boughs,
> held a dove in her two hands,
> let it fly up from the bowl she made
> as if a word had left her lips.
>
> [*Roots,* p. 87]

Mother and child, falconress and falcon, unite in the mythic act of *poesis:* a creative union of birth and death in speech, the contest of that primal tension. As George Hole wrote of "Falconress," Duncan has generated "an incestuous metaphor (I create her who creates me)."[9]

> At the babe's birth
>           the whole woman
> opens   ·   the flower bleeding,   life-lanced   ·
>           the head of the embryo
> shoved forth from its red pod,   from the pain she knows,
>           into the Child's place
>           ·   cries.
>
> [*Bow,* pp. 24–25]

That primal cry echoes the painful harmony of both mother and child, in chorus.

"My Mother Would Be a Falconress" becomes finally for me an act of memory and mourning ("I must bring back carefully"): a re-creation which is also an act of aggression, a *drawing* of blood, a portrait of the life and pain and joy of a relationship lost but obsessively present.[10] Left talking to himself, the poet resurrects an image of his mother(s) in a careful and devoted drama of affection and hostility, grief and guilt. I hear in his final words, "and would draw blood," a wish not merely to hurt, or to feed himself from her corpse, but to bring her back: a wish for re-union, for new life in an old memory. Duncan's poem is for me a desperate and magnificent attempt to re-create a commanding antagonist worthy of his love and his grief: to construct a form with which to wrestle, and a matrix in which to rest.

My own act of hypocriticism, as I've reconstructed it in these pages, seems to mirror the shape of the poem. First I moved away, to thoughts of my own mother and a specific event in my past; then I wrestled with the text, applying critical and analytic holds to pin down significance. Continually feeling the tense ambivalence of restraint and release which the poem evoked, I ultimately returned in admiration to the words, images, and emotions which the poet created and I took in. The design of my critical motions imitates the flight of the poet's falcon. Finally the falcon becomes an image of myself as reader and as critic (hypocritic). The poetic image subsumes and symbolizes all its participants: son, poet, poem itself, and reader, combined in and shaped by the reciprocal acts of creating and re-creating which Robert Duncan and I share, in mutual rivalry, as we share this poem.

## Notes

1. "Should not the interpreter have personae?" asks Geoffrey Hartman (*The Fate of Reading* [Chicago: University of Chicago Press, 1975], p. 10). Yes, and they are both his face and the masks he wears for each different text: devices to sound through (*persona*), which both conceal and reveal his critical features. They present the person plus his impersonation.

2. See Hartman, *The Fate of Reading,* p. xiii.

3. *The Years as Catches: First Poems (1939–1946)* (Berkeley, Calif.: Oyez Press, 1966), p. viii. Duncan's writings will be abbreviated as follows: *Bow: Bending the Bow* (New York: New Directions, 1968); *Roots: Roots and Branches* (New York: New Directions, 1964); *Truth: The Truth & Life of Myth: An Essay in Essential Autobiography* (Fremont, Mich.: Sumac Press, 1968); *Years: The Years as Catches: First Poems (1939–1946).*

4. From *Bending the Bow,* copyright © 1964, 1966, 1968 by Robert Duncan. Reprinted by permission of New Directions Publishing Corporation.

5. "μύζω (A) To make the sound μὺ μῦ or μυμῦ, to murmur with closed lips, to mutter, moan, . . . (B) to drink with closed lips, to suck in. . . ." From Liddell and Scott, *Greek-English Lexicon* (London, 1897); quoted by Duncan as a preface to *Truth.*

6. Technically, in falconry the term *falcon* refers to the female hawk (frequently a

peregrine). The male hawk is a "tiercel." I find further confusions between falcon and falconress, son and mother, in lines 13–14, in the mutuality of wills.

7. My third ear hears at various points in the poem a sense of the word "will," and of "pride" as well, which Duncan may be aware of. He knows Shakespeare and Renaissance bawdry, and is a thorough student of language and etymology. A meaning of "will" as "sexual organ" (see Eric Partridge, *Shakespeare's Bawdy*, or Sonnet 135) adds anatomical sense to a line like "far, far beyond the curb of her will" (51). It gives bodily substance to the general theme of separation, liberation, rebellion, by providing an explicit image of the act of birth: beyond the confines of her womb. Duncan's poetry is frequently a poetry of the body.

8. Duncan has written of the "homoerotic lure" of poetry, which he says agrees with "Freud's concept of the underlying disturbed and disturbing bisexuality of man's nature": see his remarks on George Barker's poetry, in *Years*, pp. ii–iii. Considering Duncan's knowledge of Freud, I doubt that the piece of psychoanalytic interpretation I've put forward will be unfamiliar to him.

9. See Norman Holland and Murray Schwartz, "The Delphi Seminar," *College English* 36 (1975): 798.

10. A poem in *Roots*, "Cover Images" (pp. 53–55), bears on this aspect of "Falconress." The poem enacts a psychic drama of reaching for an Edenic mother, but the impulse is distorted by primal rage against her for implicit sexual transgressions which exclude the child. The poet creates an image, a painting-poem, of his mother, then does violence to it as he draws, inflicting injuries and bruises with each stroke. Finally her dismembered, "hackt," "partly devourd" body becomes his own. It is a "hideous vision," yet it reveals the "damnd root" of Duncan's art. Rage against the loved and lost mother turns into an attack upon himself.

# Rhetoric and Literature

# The Economics of the Literary Text

## Daniel Stempel
### University of Hawaii at Manoa

I

THE New Formalism is not the legitimate heir of the New Criticism. Historical scholarship and the New Criticism negotiated an uneasy truce because the New Critics never claimed the authority of a systematic methodology; indeed, they scorned any imputation of scientific rigor. In contrast, contemporary formalism, rooted in the procedures of structural linguistics, has expanded beyond its origins by appropriating models from all the sciences, physical, biological, and human. Of all these the economic paradigm might have been expected to provide a last redoubt for embattled historicism, but structuralism and the mutations that have developed from it have succeeded in petrifying even Marxist theory into a complex aesthetic object, isolated by its total autonomy not only from past and future, but from any possible reference to historical actuality.[1] And now two intrepid critics have planted the banner of the New Formalism well within the walls of the fortress of economics. Marc Shell's *The Economy of Literature*[2] and Kurt Heinzelman's *The Economics of the Imagination*[3] have linked the language of literature and the language of economics through common rhetorical elements and structures. Both books are impressive, not only because they exhibit the mastery of a discipline outside the customary limits of literary studies, but because their application of that discipline to readings of texts is sensitive and intelligent. And yet, despite my admiration of the range and subtlety of their practical criticism, I sense that much of it may be a juggling act of rhetorical

97

*Klügelei* which dazzles us with arguments spinning in thin air above the abyss of sophistry. The theoretical foundation of their work, which rests on certain assumptions about the formal constitution of literary texts, is questionable; it satisfies neither the simple requirements of ordinary logic nor the need to demonstrate clearly the role of tropes in literary discourse.

"Literary works," Shell posits flatly, "are composed of small tropic exchanges or metaphors, some of which can be analyzed in terms of signified economic content and all of which can be analyzed in terms of economic form. In these two kinds of analysis, words and verbal tropes constitute the principal focus." He extends this mode of "tropic exchange" to include "large structures," such as plots, and concludes, "literary works, then, are composed of both small and large tropic exchanges" (p. 7). Summing up, Shell describes the "subject matter" of his "thoughtful economy of literature" as the "comprehension of thought and matter" and its goal: "to show how literary and philosophical fictions (perhaps even our own) can help us to understand and to change the tyranny of our world" (p. 10). In a similar, though less Promethean, manner Heinzelman outlines his method and its aims: "By analyzing the economic forms of poetic discourse and the poetics of economic discourse simultaneously, as equally significant and instructive exertions of the imagination, we may see how the development of the political economy changes the idea of the imagination and how, through the further labor of the imagination—through its expression in poetry—economic discourse is forced to speak in more responsive ways" (p. 11). Heinzelman's summary suggests that his criticism moves within the bounds of the hermeneutic school of suspicion, to use Ricoeur's term; he is defining the operations of a set of "secret terms":

> We are speaking, then, of two phenomena: (1) "imaginative economics," the way in which economic systems are structured, by means of the imagination, upon what are essentially fictive concepts—including, ultimately, "the economy" itself—and (2) "poetic economics," the way in which literary writers use this fictive economic discourse, this body of systematized knowledge, as an ordering principle in their own work. *The Economics of the Imagination* will seek to identify the coincidence of these two "economics" by showing how the "secret terms" of economic discourse encroach upon moral and aesthetic issues—indeed upon the whole life of the imagination. [Pp. 11–12]

Heinzelman's method is essentially the same as Shell's: "Ultimately, poetry shows economics as a form of metaphorization which partakes of the mythic force of poetry itself and which, therefore, may be used in poetry as a schematic method of defining poetry's own ontological status" (pp. 12–13).

Both studies, then, begin with the premise that literary and economic discourse intersect in common elementary constituents, tropes or metaphorical exchanges, and that fictions are large structures of tropes that organize both kinds of texts. While this may seem axiomatic to certain schools of critical analysis, others, like myself, find it unconvincing. By the same kind of reasoning one could argue that all tapestries are composed of colored threads and that therefore a tapestry is a multicolored large thread or rope. Further, the argument that fictions are employed in both economics and literature and that, as a result, one can be translated into the other, is no more convincing than the assumption that, since English and French share a common alphabet, if one can read English, one can read French. We must clarify the relation of tropes and fictions in literary texts before the kind of analysis attempted in these studies can be extended to other forms of discourse. I propose to reverse their procedure and begin with an examination of how such texts are constituted through architectonic structures rather than through an aggregation of elementary units of metaphor.

Literary discourse, like all discourse, appears in a space. Its constitution is not governed by the *tropos* but by the *topos,* the locus of possible statements; the topos locates a text without specifying the final form of its language. Aristotle defined it as the space of an argument that must be developed through dialectic, not syllogistic logic: "The purpose of the present treatise *(Topics)* is to discover a method by which we shall be able to reason from probable propositions *(endoxa)* about any problem set before us and shall ourselves, when sustaining an argument, avoid saying anything self-contradictory."[4] For Quintilian topoi are "sedes argumentorum, in quibus latent, ex quibus sunt petenda," the secret places where arguments hide, and from which they must be drawn forth.[5] The topos of classical rhetoric is analogous to Wittgenstein's definition of logical space:

> The truth-conditions of a proposition determine the range that it leaves open to the facts.
> (A proposition, a picture, or a model is, in the negative sense, like a solid body that restricts the freedom of movement of others, and,

in the positive sense, like a space bounded by solid substance in which there is room for a body.)

A tautology leaves open to reality the whole—the infinite whole—of logical space; a contradiction fills the whole of logical space leaving no point of it for reality. Thus neither of them can determine reality in any way.

A tautology's truth is certain, a proposition's possible, a contradiction's impossible.[6]

The topos or locus has a separate and different function in the art of memory of classical oratory: the topos as memory place. This ancillary use inverts the usual role of the topos in discourse. Instead of opening logical space, it occupies and marks a space in a nonlogical or even nonverbal structure, a semiotic template that encodes a message from the orator to himself. In this process a curious shift takes place. The metaphorical use of topos or locus as logical space becomes an actual, though purely mental, location, where *images* are placed so that they can be recalled in the order of the mnemonic structure.

> The artificial memory includes loci and images. By loci I mean such scenes as are naturally or artificially set off on a small scale, complete and conspicuous, so that we can grasp and embrace them easily by the natural memory—for example, a house, an intercolumnar space, a recess, an arch, or the like. An image is, as it were, a figure, mark, or portrait of the object we wish to remember; for example, if we wish to recall a horse, a lion, or an eagle, we must place its image in a definite locus.[7]

Although the mnemonic image is produced by and for the speaker to facilitate recall, while the images associated with the literary text are linked to its reading by someone other than the writer, the way in which mnemonic images are put together as wholes and linked to an architectonic structure helps to unravel the interaction of textual organization, mental images, and figurative language. The relation of the memory image to the text is so tightly controlled that we can trace that interaction through each constitutive step, avoiding the misleading identification of image (here used strictly in the sense of mental image) and linguistic figure. C. Day Lewis's definition of the poetic image as "a picture made out of words" is characteristic of the theory of verbal mimesis, the belief that the poetic image is a "fusion of sense and sensa," that in some way language acquires the characteristics of that which it represents and becomes "iconic."[8]

But this fusion is merely confusion. As Pierre Francastel argues, words do not make pictures, pictures do not make words.
"We have seen in recent years," he writes, "this split demonstrated between those who see and those who listen or speak.
Dominated by the illusion of the primacy of language, reflections on film in particular have revealed how a conception of
the life of the mind dominated solely by verbal thinking is
incapable of explaining other systems of signification."[9] Francastel finds in the "figurative" system (the system of *pictorial*
images) a triple structuring, the arrangement of objects and
spaces within a visible whole, while linguistic analysis is based
on a double articulation (phoneme/morpheme) that subdivides
a single act of mind into levels of immediate constituents.
"Founded on this mechanism of a triple institution, the
figurative systems are no less imaginary nor do they make less
of an appeal to memory than language. It is in the memory, in
effect, that are organized and integrated the diverse categories
of figurative objects corresponding to diverse degrees of brute
experience and socialized experience—where the objects of
civilization come to birth—for which reason the decoding of
material signs integrated at the level of imaginary places and
fixed on a fixed support makes possible intellection and reading" (p. 154). Instead of referring art to a linguistic model,
Francastel stresses its autonomous organization as a system of
signs: "On ne peut assimiler l'art à une philologie" (p. 31).
    The reverse is also true—language cannot be assimilated to
art. Francastel's crucial distinction allows us to understand the
unique form of mediation represented by the traditional memory system of loci and images. It is not a true linguistic system.
Instead, it utilizes the triple institution of visual systems, "the
decoding of material signs integrated at the level of imaginary
places and fixed on a fixed support." The link between the
rhetorical figures of language and mental images is referential,
not mimetic. To make this clearer I shall borrow some prefixes
from Freud's model of the mind for a non-Freudian theory of
literary language. I define the literary text as the con-text, a set
of compossible statements unified by the structure of a recognizable literary work of art. This is the text presented to the
reader. It refers in multiple ways to semantic sub-texts, linguistic texts that share a common theme or are part of a common
oeuvre or a common genre. The pre-text is not linguistic; it is as
yet unverbalized experience, what can be said. A visual experience can be reported or described, but it cannot be reproduced

in language. Wittgenstein's aphorism has a broader application than was originally intended: "What *can* be shown, *cannot* be said."[10] Beyond these texts, resisting all visual or verbal definition, is the un-text, Boehme's *Ungrund,* Wittgenstein's *Unaussprechliches,* Heidegger's *Sein.* But to account for the metaphorical content of the poetic text, we need another set of prefixes to describe a mediating function, similar to that of mnemonic images, that occurs *after* the constitution of ordinary language and *prior* to the constitution of the literary text.

What I am attempting to describe is not the actual process of the development of the poetic text; it is the constitution of that text. To illustrate the distinction: if I say I am going to fly to Europe from Honolulu, it is a necessary conclusion that I must cross the Pacific. That is essential for the constitution of my itinerary. But my actual route—east, west, or over the pole—cannot be determined from my statement. In this sense, then, I can say that all subtextuality (intertextuality) functions as ordinary language for the poetic text, as paraphrase or even as quotation. It is that "virtual" language which Gérard Genette views as operative beneath the "real" language of the actual poetic text.[11] The "real" language is generated from the "virtual" language through the mediation of visual (nonverbal) images created from sub-texts. In relation to these sub-texts they are post-textual, but they are also prior to the real text, i.e., they provide a nonverbal origin whose source lies in language and whose product is the fusion of logical structure and linguistic deviation. That novelty which allows the mnemonic image to govern recall is also essential for the poetic image. As Gaston Bachelard points out, "by its novelty a poetic image sets in motion the entire linguistic mechanism. The poetic image places us at the origin of the speaking being."[12] From the reader's angle, "the poetic image is an emergence from language, it is always a little above the language of signification" (p. xxiii). The use of imagination as part of the *technē* of oratory is a limited application of the same power that acts as *poiēsis* in the literary text. Just as the orator produces *imagines* to recall the order and substance of his argument, so the poet creates images that mediate between sub-text and con-text. In the poetic text, as Bachelard phrases it, "all memory has to be reimagined" (p. 175).

The mediating image, which is a mental image, is not a reproduction of sense experience. Any question involving its correspondence with reality or its strength or weakness is irrelevant; it is not a perception, it is a construct, a model for reference.[13] The way in which it reorganizes language falls neatly between Wittgenstein's two analyses of linguistic usage: language as "bildliche Darstellung," pictorial presentations, and language as a game. His picture theory proposes models constructed by mapping relations; the model is not a reproduction, it is a projection, a scale model. His game theory, in contrast, emphasizes free play through changes in linguistic rules or even violations of them, permitting the individualizing of language, the production of discourse that is unique, recognizable, and memorable—a physiognomy, not a map.

Rhetorical figures are not necessarily tied to images. If metaphors, as Ricoeur claims, are juxtapositions linked by a polarity or tension of similarity and difference, metaphorical language may be generated by intertextual combinations, as in the allusive poetry of Eliot and Pound, bypassing the level of poetic imagery or passing it on to the reader.[14] In all instances, however, rhetorical figures must include those two essentials posited by C. Perelman and L. Olbrechts-Tyteca in their *New Rhetoric:* "In order that there may be a figure, the presence of two characteristics would seem essential: a discernible structure, independent of the content, in other words a form (which may, under the divisions recognized by modern logicians, be syntactic, semantic, or pragmatic), and a use that is different from the normal manner of expression and, consequently, attracts attention."[15]

I shall use the term *schemata* for the "discernible structure" of ordered discourse and *schema* for each propositional step in that order. The rhetorical figure or trope that instantiates each schema takes its place in the structure and, at the same time, *realizes* the schema through a novel and memorable juxtaposition of words. Again, the modest example of the art of memory demonstrates the manner in which an image is bound to an ordered frame which it individualizes for purposes of recognition and recall. In the literary text, however, the image determines the form of language, not the form of memory. The relation of schema to trope is that of the sculptor's armature to the clay that fleshes it out. The original sense of schemata is the series of postures of the body in gymnastics or in acting; the schema is a position, an attitude, in a sequence of movements; the trope gives it a face and a figure.

Almost every writer on images from the author of the *Rhetorica ad Herennium* to Gaston Bachelard has listed two requirements for memorable images: first, they must be novel and striking, qualities achieved primarily through action ("aliquid agentes imagines," *ad Herennium,* p. 220); second, they preserve their novelty when they are kept in an order the mind can retrace ("But this will be essential—again and again to run over rapidly in the mind all the original loci in order to refresh the images," ibid.). The order of memory locations is linked to a room or public building through which one walks in imagination, placing and retrieving items. Like the cardinal number system, it does not resemble what it organizes; it lends itself to any sequence.

But, as Frances Yates suggests, the use of *ficta loca* in medieval and renaissance memory techniques, imagined places such as heaven or hell, transformed the semiotic frame into a semantic order.[16] In the *Divine Comedy* the image not only lends its power of representation to the structure in which it is embedded, it borrows its interpretation from that structure. The sense of the trope is governed by the fictive order that locates all tropes. As Bachelard warns, it is not the function of the poetic image to free language from the order of discourse; the isolated image induces a mere solipsistic reverie: "The dreamer drifts away. A true poet is not satisfied with this evasive imagination. He wants imagination to be a *voyage.* Thus each poet owes us his *invitation to the voyage. . . .* If the initial image is well chosen, it is am impulsion to a well-defined dream, to an imaginary life that will have real laws of successive images, really vital meaning."[17]

The development of memory systems in the Renaissance into models of cosmic order, which Frances Yates traces in the work of Lull, Camillo, Bruno, and Fludd, strengthened the control of architectonic order over images and their linguistic representations. By manipulating the symbolic elements of these models, one could determine all possible structures of reality. This practice, common to both science and magic in an age when they were often combined, focused attention on the language of possibility as opposed to the language of description. Yates believes that Leibniz's search for a *characteristica universalis,* a logic with the rigor of mathematical symbols and functions, marks the culmination of this tradition as well as the beginning of modern logic. It was Leibniz who began the task of clarifying the distinction between language as mimesis, the representation of actuality, and language as logic, the representation of possibility.

This distinction was already implicit in Aristotle's classification of the topoi of argumentation: "Most of the things about which we make decisions, and into which we therefore inquire, present us with alternative possibilities."[18] The speaker who intends to persuade his listeners to a course of action must have at his command "propositions about the possible and the impossible, and about whether a thing has or has not occurred, will or will not occur" (p. 34). The lines of reasoning developed from topoi are developed by dialectic; they are not confined to any particular subject or area of investigation. As the dialectic moves from point to point, it creates a logical structure which, like all "fictive" structures, is mimetic only in a limited and strictly defined sense. It is not an imitation of actuality, since it can develop an argument on nonactualized premises or indeed from counterfactuals, such as probable impossibilities. Nor is it totally independent of actuality; its premises, even if they are to be refuted, are drawn from the common experience of all.[19]

Literary texts, even when they are designedly mimetic or "realistic," are always constructions of possible worlds of discourse; their intrinsic coherence (the con-text) is the ground of their autonomy. Their internal order is comparable to the order of dialectic discourse in argumentation: it is a governing order that both frames and interacts with images to produce the language of literature. It is not constituted by images nor does it constitute them. It opens the logical space of the text for them, giving them a location they fill with their own freedom. Aristotle's rhetorical topoi and Curtius's literary topoi perform a common function—they open the space of a text with a probable premise, a commonplace or even a cliché, from which *inventio* develops the *dispositio* of propositional statements, the logical progression of schemata, and realizes them through *elocutio,* the interaction of schema and trope in figurative language. The topos can be both cliché and archetype, as Curtius suggests, because it is the *beginning* of discourse.[20] It is the logic of possible statement that gives the literary text both its order and its freedom.

The architectonic function of the order of possible statements in literary texts is now a subject of intense investigation by linguists and philosophers, but the basic theory was outlined around 1740 by two Swiss aestheticians, J. J. Bodmer and J. J. Breitinger. Using as their premise Leibniz's distinction between the truth of existential propositions and the truth of possible propositions, they redefined the term *imitation* so that it no longer indicated a correspondence between language and actuality. Breitinger formulated this in an axiom: "For there are two categories of truth in Nature: one exists only in the world which is present to us; the other, however, occurs only in the world of possible things. The former we call the historical and the latter the poetic truth."[21]

Breitinger rejected the classical dogma that allows the poet to improve upon nature, insisting with Leibniz that this is the best of all possible worlds and therefore cannot be improved. But the poet is not limited to things as they are. His possible worlds are constructs, extrapolations from the known to the unknown, not independent alternative realities. "The improbable in poetry always possesses a possibility, to put it simply, which is grounded in the power of the Creator of Nature. It is improbable and impossible with regard to certain specific conditions and circumstances with which it may appear only when it contradicts them, although it would not be impossible in other circumstances and conditions" (1:135). Breitinger's emphasis is on an internal teleology rather than a structure imposed on the text by an external reality:

> Because the present arrangement of the world of real things is not absolutely necessary, the Creator might have produced beings of a totally different kind for different ends, linked them together in a different order, and prescribed wholly different laws for them. Now since poetry is an imitation of creation and nature, not only in the real but also in the possible, its composition, which is a form of creation, must ground its probability either in its correspondence with the established laws and course of nature of the present time or in the powers of Nature which she might have exercised for other ends, according to our theory. In both instances the probability consists in this: that the circumstances coincide with the purpose, that they are grounded in each other, and that no contradiction between them may be demonstrated. [1:136–37]

A fictive structure is one where possible premises serve as topoi from which to develop a self-consistent order; all elements are not merely possible but compossible. This semantic order presents "truth" solely through coherence, not through a correspondence with actuality nor with a "higher" form of reality. Although it may contradict experience, it does not contradict itself. In *Gulliver's Travels* a change of a single premise, Gulliver's size in relation to his surroundings, creates the possible worlds of Lilliput and Brobdingnag. To sum up, the literary text is a structure of compossible statements that do not contradict each other, except where the generating axiom of these statements is contradiction itself, as in riddling songs (here the elements conform to the principle of selection and preserve the unity of the text).

The attempt to reduce this order to a juxtaposition of tropes or to tropic paradigms is the result of a failure to understand that the constitution or production of a text is not necessarily congruent with the analysis of a text. Structuralism (and its offshoots) assumes that the language of texts is a material cause, the combination of immediate constituents of sound and meaning in accordance with mechanisms of distribution, or a formal cause, the crystalization of mechanisms of patterning and distortion. But we must view it as an efficient cause and ask how it works and what it is doing. Only when we place its elements within the context of the entire process are we able to distinguish the specific contributions of premises, schemata, and tropes; the study of a text must trace the inner history of a functioning structure. To determine how the work "works" or does not work, the reader must intuit the interplay of form and metaphor, using models only when they are truly congruent with textual form, not as postulated parallels or hidden codes or Baconian lists of binary oppositions.

Economic models are no more privileged among fictive structures in literary texts than the strange and charming fictions of nuclear physics. They are *bildliche Darstellungen,* projections. Perhaps the most pervasive principle in economic thought is that of balance or equilibrium, but it shares this principle with every model based on an ideal closed system. From the household economy of Xenophon to the complex models of current theorists, whether the primary function of the economy is distribution or reciprocity or exchange, the common aim is to maintain, regain, or pursue equilibrium. Aristotle's condemnation of the accumulation of wealth is a logical extension of his biological model, the organism whose metabolism must be kept in balance. Too much and it dies or becomes monstrous; too little and it cannot survive. For each household and each polis there is an optimum size that is maintained by an equilibrium between income and consumption.

Michel Foucault, with his genius for grasping the essential core of problematics, has suggested that three models dominate the human sciences, the modern disciplines whose subject is man and his activities: the biological model of the interaction of function and norm; the economic model of the conflict of needs and desires and their regulation through pragmatic rules; and the linguistic model of the systematic organization of meaning.[22] Although Foucault presents these models as categories of epistemological organization, they are paradigms of constitution fundamental to phenomenological analysis: "Instead of the single experiences being analyzed and compared, described and classified, all treatment of detail is governed by the 'teleological' view of its function in making 'synthetic unity' possible."[23] These constitutive paradigms are not mutually exclusive; they interlock and can be used to interpret each other as well as the constitutive structures of discourse. As interpretive tools, they are not limited to the periodization of historical discourse; these normative forms of intentionality are always present in our cultural consciousness, though not always present to consciousness.

The three plays of Sophocles' Oedipus cycle, which, as Freud and others have recognized, exercise a canonical priority as literary texts within a wide range of interpretation, are perfect exemplars of the latent teleology of each of Foucault's paradigms. *Oedipus Tyrannus* is structured by the biological model; its problem is one of disordered function in ruler and polis. To restore the norm the city of Thebes must excise the source of its infection, Oedipus himself. In the *Antigone* the problem is economic, one of conflict and rule. The clash of loyalties cannot be resolved by divine justice; it is a pragmatic submission to the rule of tragic necessity that restores the equilibrium of the state. The linguistic model shapes the last of these plays to be written, *Oedipus at Colonus*. Oedipus' assumption or descent into the realm of the gods opens with thunder but concludes in silence, the silence of language degree zero, a gesture that points to the unity of the un-text. It does not give a meaning to the suffering of Oedipus; it makes it meaningful.

II

How can an economic reading shaped by constitutive paradigms, not by the model of a Rubik's cube of metaphors neatly aligned through a deft twisting of the text, bring to light the buried wealth of imaginative structure in a familiar text? Wordsworth's "Michael: A Pastoral Poem" offers itself as an ideal text for an economic reading, not only because its content is a problematic of loss and gain but because its language is stripped of metaphor. This allows us to bracket one of the two characteristics of rhetorical discourse defined in *The New Rhetoric:* a text written in ordinary language does not call attention to its difference from common usage. This bracketing leaves us free to examine the other requirement of rhetoric: a "discernible structure" that may be pragmatic, syntactic, or semantic.

The pragmatic form of "Michael" is the literal text, the words of the narrator addressing a listener.[24] As a native-born guide, versed in local lore, he is explaining to a visitor the significance of the "straggling heap of unhewn stones" (l. 17) in Greenhead Ghyll. For him it is an emotional landmark, the site and symbol of the tale that stirred his earliest consciousness of human suffering. Now, as an adult, he has gathered all that can be learned about Michael from those who knew him. But the narrator is a poet as well as a regional historian. He is not Michael's heir, as Geoffrey Hartman has suggested, but, in a strict sense, the executor of his estate; his self-imposed duty is to render an accounting, as well as an account, of the straggling heap of facts that constitute the long life of Michael. His poetic accounting sums these facts up as a pathetic tale of a life of unremitting labor crowned by misfortune, "a history / Homely and rude" (ll. 34–35).

Skillfully stressing the pastoral elements of Michael's labor, he links it to the pattern of the traditional pastoral, the life of simple needs that finds its satisfaction in the round of daily and seasonal tasks. His description of Michael gives him heroic stature, identifying him with the landscape in which he labors. Not only has he been shaped by the hills, he is projected back on them, a figure larger than life, like the Shepherd of *The Prelude:* "him I have descried in distant sky, / A solitary object and sublime, / Above all height!" (8.271–73). Michael is also magnified by temporal distance. The narrator has never known him personally; his reconstruction of Michael's life is based on a mixture of local legend and hearsay.

The narrator suggests that the value of the tale, in *his* telling, lies in its ability to transform "random" and "imperfect" thoughts "on man, the heart of man, and human life" into an aesthetic form, "a history / Homely and rude . . . / For the delight of a few natural hearts" (ll. 33, 35–36) and also as an inspiration for young poets who will inherit his role as local bard. But his accounts do not balance. He shows us a man who has led an exemplary life crushed by unmotivated and un-merited catastrophe; if we are left to conclude that it teaches the ennobling of man by nature and his corruption in the city, then the poem is crudely sentimental, extracting a surplus of feeling from a minimal significance, a trite contrast. There is a distance between the narrator and his subject, Michael, that is more than temporal. It is the aesthetic distance between the poet and his poem, which projects a cold calculation of re-sponse rather than the expression of fellow-feeling that one would expect of a local poet; he separates himself from the shepherds, "men / Whom I already loved;—not verily / For their own sakes, but for the fields and hills / Where was their occupation and abode" (ll. 23–26), and slants his narration "for the sake / Of youthful Poets, who among these hills / Will be my second self when I am gone" (ll. 37–39).

Whatever Wordsworth's original intention may have been, the pragmatic form of "Michael," as a sentimental tale of rural misfortune, elicited the immediate response the narrator ex-pected of his listener, a response Wordsworth himself noted with pride: "This poem has, I know, drawn tears from the eyes of more than one, persons well acquainted with the manners of the 'Statesmen,' as they are called, of this country; and, moreover, persons who never wept, in reading verse, before." His conclusion is revealing: "This is a favourable augury for me."[25] Perhaps it was, but not for the poem, doomed to a reading as a sentimental document of romantic feeling.

The modern reader, however, senses a strength in the poem that lifts it out of its institutionalized interpretation and under-mines the dominance of its pragmatic form. The three forms of rhetorical discourse, the pragmatic, the syntactic, and the se-mantic, solicit different modes of assent from the reader.[26] The only assent required for a pragmatic structure is one of atten-tion or recognition: "That's what X says to Y," for example. No judgments are required because the statements are speech-acts in specific contexts. Syntactic statements appear in the context of a closed system of signs, a semiotic, in which all signs are interpreted through other signs. Here the response of assent is

"That's right," the acceptance of a total consistency of the statement with its logical context. Semantic statements are (ideally)
both meaningful in the syntactic order and referential to a
nonlinguistic world of things. The response of assent to a semantic proposition is "That's true." To borrow two useful
terms from Hegel, the *certainty* of a literary text is measured by
its syntactic coherence; the *truth* of a literary text is determined
by its points of congruence with actuality.

If the narrative of "Michael" is accepted without interpretation, it fails to meet the first of these criteria; no real connection
is made between any of the events of the poem and, in particular, the crucial link between Michael's character and Luke's
failure is passed over. Modern interpretations have attempted
to deal with these weaknesses by imposing a strong syntactic
model on the text within whose structure the narration can
function as an element of the text, rather than as the text itself.
Critical opinion seems to favor two approaches, the generic and
the mythical. Since Wordsworth himself labels it "A Pastoral
Poem," critics organize it in terms of the conventions of that
tradition and use the generic form of the pastoral poem as a
model. Others, noting the markers "shepherd," "patriarch,"
"covenant," and the simple chronology recast the narrative in
the mold of biblical parallels, as a retelling of archetypal myth.
But the semiotic closure demanded by the literary text is not
supplied by these borrowed forms. At best, the reader is offered a choice of a mutant form of the pastoral DNA or a
ritualized celebration of the suffering of a rural Job. The economy of the text remains unbalanced.

The measure of success in interpretation, if one takes the
literary text as *complete* discourse, not as the sum of metaphor, is
the approximation of total compossibility of statements. The
best of all possible interpretations, as the Leibnizian critics suggested, proposes an architectonic order of discourse with a
maximum of coherence and a minimum of irrelevance. (There
are texts, of course, in which irrelevance is relevant, as in the
pragmatic structure of stream-of-consciousness interior monologue.) If we look closely at *what* the narrator is saying and
break up the order in which he places the sequence of events,
the syntactic structure reveals a pattern of causality that underlies both Michael's loss of economic independence and Luke's
defection.

The financial debt Michael takes over from his brother's son is actually a repayment of a moral debt he owes his brother. Like Oedipus, Michael is unaware of the crime he has committed against his closest blood relatives; it is a guilt passed down from eldest son to eldest son, not inherited guilt but the guilt of inheritance. Michael's property has come to him through primogeniture, which preserves the integrity of the land at the expense of the integrity of the family. As Adam Smith observed, "nothing can be more contrary to the real interest of a numerous family than a right which, in order to enrich one, beggars all the rest of the children."[27] Seven years before he wrote "Michael" Wordsworth attacked "the unnatural monster of primogeniture" and blamed it for the "depopulation of the country."[28] Michael's nephew is in trade because his father was forced off the land by Michael's inheritance of the family property. This movement from land to trade was so common that one younger son who had made that move commented that by 1796 the northern counties had become "quite a manufactory for Bankers' and Merchants' clerks."[29]

As in the Oedipean economy of function and norm, reciprocity imposes a grim justice in order to right the balance of the syntactic structure. When Michael succeeded to the property at the age of twenty-four, it was burdened with debt equal to half its value, which he paid off by the time he was forty. When, at eighty-four, Michael assumes his nephew's debt, it amounts to the same proportion of his property as the original debt, "little less / Than half his substance" (ll. 216–17). But the burden of his financial responsibility is not enough to offset the moral debt of his inheritance. He must also lose his son to the city to which he has exiled his brother and his brother's children. This is the real balancing of accounts which, as Georg Lukács has suggested, is the syntactic form of all tragedy: the tragic hero is "handed the bill" *(wird die Rechnung präsentiert)* for a sum of events he has not initiated but in which he has been the prime mover of all that has happened.[30]

Neither Michael nor Luke is an innocent victim of capricious fortune. Michael, like Oedipus, stubbornly perseveres in that tragic virtue which is the hallmark of his character. Throughout the countryside his household is famed for its unflagging industry; the light in their cottage burns so late that it is named "The Evening Star." Although the narrator prefers to present Michael as a shepherd, he is a farmer as well. While Isabel spins wool and flax into thread, he and Luke repair farm tools used for grain and hay: "sickle, flail, or scythe" (l. 108). Michael is not a patriarchal herdsman; he is a successful statesman. Using the resources of his land for profit, he has made his farm and flocks *pay*. Luke was not born until he was sixty-six, but there is no hint that his way of life was different during the quarter of a century when he was neither in debt nor providing for an heir. His character, the narrator assures us, has always been the same: "His bodily frame had been from youth to age / Of an unusual strength: his mind was keen, / Intense and frugal, apt for all affairs" (ll. 43–45).

The fact that Michael was accepted as the guarantor of his nephew's credit long before the events narrated in the poem suggests that he was the master of a prosperous farm that yielded more than enough to support his small household. Michael's fear of indebtedness is so overpowering that his immediate reaction to the news of his nephew's ruin is to think the unthinkable: "it seemed / The Shepherd's sole resource to sell at once / A portion of his patrimonial fields. / Such was his first resolve; he thought again, / And his heart failed him (ll. 222–26). But to shoulder the burden of debt again and pass it on to his son, as his parents had done, seems equally unthinkable. His solution is to send Luke to the city, where money can be made quickly: "the land / Shall not go from us, and it shall be free; / He shall possess it, free as is the wind / That passes over it" (ll. 244–47). Michael has no word of sympathy for his nephew: "An evil man / That was, and made an evil choice, if he / Were false to us; and if he were not false, / There are ten thousand to whom loss like this / Had been no sorrow" (ll. 236–40). Since his nephew was a man of "ample means" (l. 212), the sum, which amounts to almost half of Michael's property, must be a relatively large one, reenforcing the conclusion that Michael was far better off than his neighbors. Michael does not mean that there are ten thousand statesmen who are wealthy enough to absorb such a loss; he is referring to a matter of common knowledge: that the holdings of the statesmen were normally encumbered with debt, and that a debt amounting to half the value of the property would be, as he suggests, nothing out of the ordinary for the average yeoman.

But the crucial point, which the narrator does not stress, is that Michael is not an average yeoman. He has paid off his inherited debt, amassed enough capital to plow and plant his fields, and is expanding the range of his grazing land by building a sheepfold near remote Greenhead Ghyll. Michael's decision to send Luke to the city is not forced upon him by the possibility of the loss of his land; after he has lost Luke and Luke's earnings, he does not sell his land. He continues to work it, although it is presumably burdened by debt, and it remains unsold until the death of Isabel, ten years later. Michael's choice is between Luke's presence at home, their common labor as son and father in the pursuit of the "certainty of honorable gain" (l. 73), and money needed to pay off the debt. Michael, not his nephew, makes an "evil choice." By sending Luke off to the city, he has made a younger brother of his son. He values the integrity of his property, not the integrity of his family.

Michael, the narrator's simple-hearted Shepherd, is the immediate ancestor of Tennyson's Northern Farmer (New Style), who cautions, "proputty, proputty sticks, an' proputty, proputty graws." Luke, like the Northern Farmer's son, is advised to "goa wheer munny is." Wordsworth was well aware that the consolidation of small holdings into large farms had been going on for decades, long before industrialization had come to the North.[31] In "Michael," if we assume that the narrator is as old as the author was in 1800, the events must have taken place in the decade of the 1760s, a period when cottage industry was still the norm. But the growth of population, which had begun much earlier, had already destroyed the precarious balance between subsistence farming and single-family ownership. While most statesmen sold out, sank further into debt, or abandoned the land, others, like Michael, increased the productivity of their holdings so that they could acquire enough capital to invest in the expansion of cultivation and husbandry.

If Michael earned enough to pay off his inherited debt in sixteen years, surely he earned much more in the following forty-four years, with the aid of Isabel and Luke. As a class, the statesmen were doomed, not only by their failure but by their success. While traditional Dalesmen preferred to raise sheep and neglected the land, others expanded their holdings and prospered during the decades of rising farm prices that began in the early 1780s. In 1790 an observer in Cumberland commented on the inevitable result: "The rust of poverty and ignorance is gradually wearing off. Estates are bought up into fewer hands; and the poorer sort of people remove into towns, to gain a livelihood by handicrafts and commerce."[32] If Michael had simply accepted the burden of debt and kept Luke on the land, Luke might have been able to say to his son, as the Northern Farmer does, "Feyther run oop to the farm, and I runs oop to the mill,/And I'll run oop to the brig."

Despite the narrator's intention, as a self-proclaimed local bard, to reduce "Michael" to a sentimental pastoral tale, it remains a history rooted in fact. His recital of misfortune piled on misfortune suppresses an organized syntactic unity whose connections are provided by the linkage of references to a semantic substructure, the real world. The narrator can slant the facts but he cannot change them. The surface contrast of idyllic country and corrupt city conceals the institutionalized injustice of primogeniture that gives Michael the land and sends his brother off to the city. This injustice is never mentioned in the poem, but it is the source of the imbalance that creates the movement of an inner economy which moves inexorably toward the restoration of equilibrium. The catastrophe that reverses Michael's fortunes robs him of everything he has taken from his brother's family. Viewed within the context of this pattern of tragic reciprocity, Luke's fall is not the surrender of a weak and malleable character to the temptations of the city. Luke has learned all that he knows from his father; his last lesson is that the value of money outweighs all other values because without it there can be no other values. Those "domestic affections" which Wordsworth attributed to the statesmen— "the parental affection, and the love of property, *landed* property, including the feelings of inheritance, home, and personal and family independence"—can be preserved only if Luke gives up *his* inheritance, *his* home, and *his* independence to provide the money his father requires.[33] Luke is not seduced by the false values of the city. The seed of his fall is already present in Michael's decision to sacrifice the unity of family and land on the altar of the new god—money.

The function of the pastoral myth, classical or biblical, is to convert the simple economy of the herdsman into a morality of the interdependence of man with man and man with nature. Ironically, this function is reversed in "Michael." Every moral relationship is converted into an economic relationship—there are no covenants in Michael's time and place, there are only contracts. Michael's moral responsibility for his brother's son is reduced to a debt. Michael senses no moral justice or retribution in the return of his nephew's debt to the property from which he has been exiled through Michael's inheritance. It is an inexplicable disaster, perhaps his nephew's fault, perhaps not. With an ironic magnanimity Michael announces, "I forgive him" (l. 240). His next recourse is to seek out another kinsman, who is a "prosperous man,/Thriving in trade" (ll. 249–50) and send Luke to him to "repair this loss" (l. 252). And, finally, the sheepfold, an economic object whose purpose is to expand the grazing area of Michael's flocks, becomes the "covenant" of Michael's pledge to Luke: "When thou return'st, thou in this place wilt see/A work which is not here: a covenant/'Twill be between us" (ll. 413–15). What he does not see, in his blind pursuit of economic independence, is that the covenant *is* work, shared labor, and that he has exchanged Luke's share for money. It is not Luke who breaks the covenant; it is Michael.

And yet, when the structure of myth is dissolved by the ironies of economic reality, Michael's stature as tragic hero is not diminished. The interaction of syntactic unity and semantic reference, of *mythos*, in the Aristotelian sense of the narrative logic of dramatic form, and history makes Michael the center and focus of an expanding circle of significance. He is, to use Hegel's term, a "world historical individual." As Georg Lukács argues, it is because such an individual is rooted in the semantic structure of history that he can rise into the aesthetic autonomy of syntactic form:

> If we have already seen in the complete personal devotion to a task a dramatization of life in life itself, it is clear that such a supreme case of involvement represents a high point dramatically both in life and art. In life, too, this basic personal unity between the individual, his life-work and his social content sharpens the concentrated sphere in which the "world historical individual" moves, drawing it around significant collisions which are materially linked with the realization of this life-work. The "world historical individual" has a dramatic character. He is destined by life itself to be a hero, to be the central figure in drama. [P. 119]

The narrator ignores the "significant collisions" of economic advantage and morality, but they are essential to the text. The history of an entire class reveals itself through the character of Michael; he exemplifies its changing values, its virtues, its defects, and its destiny. Nothing in the text is a matter of mere chance or artless reporting: Michael's cottage sits on a "plot of rising ground" (l. 132) where its light can be seen by "all/Who dwelt within the limits of the vale" (ll. 137–38). "The Evening

Star" not only marks the highest point of the traditional culture of the Dalesmen, it also heralds the twilight of that culture. Success and failure lead to the same end: the disappearance of the small landholder as a social class. The last eight lines present a historical closure as well as a semiotic closure. In sharp contrast to the romantic melancholy of the grove in which the Ruined Cottage survives as a monument to Margaret's sad life, nothing of Michael's life remains except the two symbols of his labor as a shepherd: the Clipping Tree and the sheepfold. The Agricultural Revolution has absorbed the rest; the cottage has been torn down and the land on which it stood has been turned into plowed fields. The text moves from *topos* to *typos*. The duration of a life is also the time of history; its rhythm brings to light the contradictions that mark the transition from one way of life to another.

There is a history of structures as well as a structure of history. The identification of historical shifts in discourse encourages the analysis of historical changes of form in literature without breaching the autonomy of the literary text. Although "Michael" has the same economic structure of reciprocity and the same self-determined closure as classical tragedy, it does not reenact an unchanging myth. Instead, it explores the tragic paradoxes of a society in transition. When Hegel, Wordsworth's contemporary, declared the most perfect tragedy was the *Antigone*, he was bringing together a new mode of discourse and a new literary form, not reviving a classical standard of excellence. The new mode of discourse was a rhetoric of analysis in which the development of meaning advances through the dissolution of the empirical proposition by a semantic surplus. The content of language contradicts and destroys the form of simple attribution. No subject and predicate are equal; no copula is a mere link. The temporary closure of logical space through contradiction forces language to move beyond and above its formal limits, transforming meaning into process, not end. The literary form demanded by this theory is one that internalizes change as a structural principle.

Thus, although the language of "Michael" consists of simple statements in the linear order of a "history homely and rude," both the statements and the order reveal themselves as inadequate, upon reflection, to their semantic content; actuality forces its way into the syntactic structure and contradicts the pragmatic structure. As the narrator moves from his self-conscious introduction to an objective recital of the grim facts, he becomes a voice captured by the events it recounts, mapping in the precise chronology of a life shattered by inexplicable change the passing of an entire community. The overbalance of unmitigated disaster imposes a burden that the turgid rhetoric of self-indulgent sentimentality cannot bear. The inner stress of contradiction reverses the text; the narrative masters the narrator and solicits its own reading, a reading that rejects his telling. In "Michael," as in the *Antigone,* irony marks the failure of recognition. In Michael, the tragic hero, history never comes to self-consciousness; it fails to recognize itself. His honesty becomes an unconscious duplicity; his unalienated labor leads to his alienation.

<h1 style="text-align:center">III</h1>

The question of method raised by the attitude of Shell and Heinzelman toward the texts they examine goes beyond the limits of the traditional quarrel between historians and formalists. The enlistment of Holy Rhetoric for the sanctification of the marriage of economics and literature confers a legitimacy that is, at best, doubtful. This uneasy alliance reflects a blurring of categories that allows a thinker as respected as Ricoeur to group Marx with Nietzsche and Freud as the "school of suspicion," which teaches that all consciousness is false consciousness. The text is a deception whose hidden meaning can be revealed only through "deciphering": "*Guile will be met by double guile.*"[34]

But "double guile" becomes a reflexive undermining of the very arguments Shell and Heinzelman make so persuasively; in search of subtle refinements of interpretation, they reach out for strained comparisons or ignore relevant information.[35] Heinzelman's effort to link labor, as an economic term, with the aesthetics of literary texts fails to recognize that "labor," like "life" and "language," is, as Foucault has suggested, one of the basic rhetorical terms of modern discourse. Unlike the terms of classical discourse, it lacks the ontological priority of derivation from an ideal origin; it can only be defined in terms of the finite discourse within which it is operative, economics, if it is to have any real significance. In the context of the discourse of language, every text, no matter how mundane, is produced by labor and requires the labor of the reader; that is essential for any act of communication.[36] Through a complex series of metaphorical equivalences, Heinzelman converts the text of "Michael" into a "property" that Wordsworth passes on to the reader as Michael wishes to pass his property on to Luke. Heinzelman sees the reader as faced with Luke's "choice," to accept or reject the labor of the poet.

> For Wordsworth, the basis of poetic value is also a contract which burdens the reader with the need to labor in order to sustain that (poetic) inheritance which is a necessary part of existence. A metaphorical law of primogeniture further entails "Michael," insofar as Wordsworth replays, in respect to the reader, Michael's role in respect to Luke. The labor bestowed upon Luke prefigures the (poet's) labor bestowed upon the reader. The poem's greatest risk is also, therefore, its greatest challenge, for it presents the reader, symbolically, with Luke's very choice. Michael's property, which is "like a book," and Wordsworth's property, which is this poem, become equivalent: each becomes vulnerable to a similar disregard, an equally crippling forfeiture. Wordsworth in fact challenges the reader to help him prove that the *labor* embodied by both of them together in the literary work is abundant recompense for the dispossession of Michael's *land*. [P. 221]

Here the text becomes the metaphorical product of a metaphorical labor that is inherited by the reader in accordance with a metaphorical primogeniture—triple guile! Heinzelman pursues the metaphor of exchange with such zeal that he does not recognize the function of primogeniture within the poem as an unjust form of *distribution,* not exchange. In brief, what he has done is to take two elements of the internal structure, primogeniture and labor, convert them into metaphorical processes, and then turn the poem inside out, externalizing it into a metaphorical exchange between writer and reader. When metaphor usurps the role of structure as process, the result is always a reification of the text, the conversion of the text into an object.

What Heinzelman's reading reveals about his approach to this text becomes clear in the light of Foucault's periodization of discourse, which distinguishes three modes of reading as well as generating texts. The Renaissance text, the book, is organized by a canonical grammar; it links all texts through the resemblance of paradigmatic figures. The Classical text, the table of names, derives its structure ultimately from the attributive statement, the proposition. The Modern text appears in the field of forces that connect and separate the polar opposites of language as pure form and language as the inadequate sign of the unknowable. Rhetoric, as I have suggested elsewhere, comes into being within this field of discourse, lending itself to both formalism and interpretation as a mode of systematic categorizing of displacement of meaning.[37]

The Renaissance text is always superior to its reading; it may be construed but it can never be adequately translated. The Classical text is congruent with its reading at that point where the logical structures of both coincide; text and reading are mutually adequate. The Modern text, as the mask of meaning, is always inferior to the reading. Since its structure is not retrievable either as the fixed order of a constant grammar or as the revelation of logic through logic, it must be read as a metaphor generated by metaphors. When the trope as mask is removed, another trope appears, and so on, in an infinite regression. Modern reading rewrites the text by reversing the order of classical rhetoric: the trope that shapes the language of the con-text by instantiating its logic is projected back into the text to convert that logic into an immanent mechanism of displacement. To borrow Heinzelman's analogy, the reader who "inherits" a text no longer feels bound by any contract. As the new owner, he is free to tear down the cottage, plow the land, and plant his favorite metaphors. The text becomes a polyvalent metaphor without a logical center, the "deconstructed" text, totally vulnerable to the whims of misprision masquerading as interpretation.

To read Marx in this way is to transform his economic history into Freudian discourse, the representation of consciousness as the surface of a field of linked automatic mechanisms, like the distribution of immediate constituents in structural linguistics, which is traversed and distorted by the vectors of an unknown energy: a surface pushed downward by repression, forced upward by sublimation, squeezed together by condensation, and stretched apart by displacement. The possibility of translating mechanism into metaphor also suggests its reversal, the translation of metaphor into mechanism, a process that dominates Freudian literary criticism. If this is the actual organization of Marx's texts, then Althusser is justified in claiming that his reading restores the unity of the text of *Das Kapital*, whose omissions and misstatements signify a hidden intention of which the author was unconscious. It is scarcely necessary to add that as a result of this failure of insight into his own methodology, Marx fell into the error of admiring Darwin, whose history of biological structures paralleled (he assumed) his history of economic structures.

While I have little inclination to engage in polemics against modern rhetorical criticism, I find it instructive and amusing, as a student of history, to trace the "lines of affinity," to use Darwin's term, that lead back from current critical practice to a common ancestor. Ezra Pound's greatest triumph, as an archaeologist of texts, was the discovery of another Rosetta stone, one that could be used to encode rather than decipher by transliterating phonetic script into hieroglyphs. Fenollosa's essay, "The Chinese Written Character as a Medium for Poetry," offered the seductive promise of a language of "visible metaphor," a perspicuous language without grammar or syntax in which all structure is the blending of separate explosions of meaning that occur when words, as metaphorical atoms, are brought close enough to reach critical mass: "Thus in all poetry a word is like a sun, with its corona and chromosphere; words crowd upon words, and enwrap each other in their luminous envelopes until sentences become clear, continuous light-bands."[38]

Hugh Kenner rightly hails this essay as the *Ars Poetica* of our age, but it introduced a method of reading as well as a method of writing.[39] "How shall we determine the metaphorical overtones of neighboring words?" Fenollosa asked, and referred the decision to the reader's ability to distinguish "a single dominant overtone [which] colors every plane of meaning." Taking three ideograms in which the sun radical is the common element, he combined them into a sentence, "Sun Rises (in the) East," claiming that he could "see" in the middle character the "single upright line . . . like the growing trunk-line of the tree sign" that appears in the last character. But that line, which is part of another radical, could never be read as an independent sign of meaning, just as the ostensive forefinger extended horizontally is never confused with the same finger raised vertically, and has a very different significance. "This," Fenollosa concludes happily, "is but a beginning, but it points the way to the method, and to the method of intelligent reading" (pp. 387–88).

The hermeneutic of this "method of intelligent reading" is properly defined as the perception of the text as an aggregate of metaphors linked by what the reader *sees* as structural unity.[40] This implicit rule seems ubiquitous in contemporary criticism, from the learned doctors of the University of Paris to the self-lacerating worshipers of the goddess Aporia at her shrine in New Haven. Rhetorical and structural critics use formal models to classify and analyze units of metaphor and their combinations; the deconstructionists approach the text as a game rather than a system, insisting that it must be played by the rules they make up as they go along. All attempt to deal with the central problem of semantic and linguistic displacement, but one group measures that displacement with a yardstick that has only one end and the other manipulates distortion by further distortion, using metaphor as metalanguage.

But perhaps they too are inheritors, not the depersonalized voices of structures without history. Kenneth Burke's dramatistic criticism is an expansion of Fenollosa's reduction of the sentence to an act centered in the verb: "the act is the very substance of the fact denoted. The agent and the subject are only limiting terms" (p. 367). The familiar equation of metaphor and mask, the emphasis on etymology as hidden metaphor—these are already present in Fenollosa's essay: "Only scholars and poets feel painfully back along the thread of our etymologies and piece together our diction, as they may, from forgotten fragments. . . . There is little or nothing in a phonetic word to exhibit the embryonic stages of its growth. It does not bear its metaphor on its face. We forget that personality once meant, not the soul, but the soul's mask" (p. 379).

Not all the ironies of history are tragic. The laughter of the Comic Spirit sounds when Fenollosa, the Horace of rhetorical reading, appeals to the authority of evolution and fulminates against the dead hand of "medieval logic": "It is impossible to represent change in this system or any kind of growth. *This is probably why the concept of evolution came so late in Europe. It could not make way until it was prepared to destroy the inveterate logic of classification*" (p. 382). As the founder of a new hermeneutic, Fenollosa could not foresee the consequences of freeing the act of reading from the task of determining the *movement* of discourse, the logic of developing form, not of classification. The freedom of the reader has become the enslavement of the text.

## Notes

1. See Louis Althusser, "Marx's Immense Theoretical Revolution," chapter 9 in *Reading Capital*, trans. Ben Brewster (London: Verso Editions, 1979): "the structure is immanent in its effects, a cause immanent in its effects in the Spinozist sense of the term, that *the whole existence of the structure consists of its effects*, in short, that the structure,

which is merely a specific combination of its peculiar elements, is nothing outside its effects" (p. 189). To someone who is familiar with the aesthetics of organic form this has a familiar ring, more Kantian than Spinozist, and particularly those sections of the *Critique of Judgment* dealing with organic form in nature (secs. 65, 66). One wonders if Althusser's metaphor of the economy as an "authorless theatre" (p. 193) is merely a clever way of rephrasing "Zweckmässigkeit ohne Zweck," purposiveness without purpose.

2. Marc Shell, *The Economy of Literature* (Baltimore, Md.: The Johns Hopkins University Press, 1977).

3. Kurt Heinzelman, *The Economics of the Imagination* (Amherst, Mass.: University of Massachusetts Press, 1980).

4. Aristotle, *Organon, Topica*, trans. E. S. Forster, 2 vols., Loeb Classical Library (Cambridge, Mass.: Harvard University Press, 1960), 2:273. I have substituted "probable propositions" for "generally accepted opinions," following the translation of Berthold Emrich, "Topik und Topoi," *Toposforschung*, ed. Max L. Baeumer (Darmstadt: Wissenschaftliche Buchgesellschaft, 1973): "aus wahrscheinlichen Sätzen."

5. *The "Institutio oratoria" of Quintilian*, trans. H. E. Butler, Loeb Classical Library (London: Heineman, 1921), 2:213.

6. Ludwig Wittgenstein, *Tractatus Logico-Philosophicus*, trans. D. F. Pears and B. F. McGuinness (London: Routledge & Kegan Paul, 1961), pp. 68–69 (4.463).

7. *Rhetorica ad Herennium*, trans. Harry Caplan, Loeb Classical Library (Cambridge, Mass.: Harvard University Press, 1954), p. 209. I have retained the Latin "locus" where Caplan translates it as "background."

8. C. Day Lewis, *The Poetic Image* (London: Jonathan Cape, 1965), p. 18; Marcus B. Hester, *The Meaning of Poetic Metaphor* (The Hague: Mouton, 1967), pp. 187–88.

9. Pierre Francastel, *La Figure et le lieu* (Paris: Gallimard, 1967), p. 105; my translation.

10. Wittgenstein, *Tractatus*, 4.1212.

11. Gérard Genette, *Figures* (Paris: Ed. du Seuil, 1966), p. 207; my translation. As Wallace Stevens writes: "The poem goes from the poet's gibberish to / The gibberish of the vulgate and back again," "Notes toward a Supreme Fiction," 9.

12. Gaston Bachelard, *The Poetics of Space*, trans. Maria Jolas (Boston: Beacon Press, 1969), p. xix.

13. See the discussion in P. N. Furbank, *Reflections on the Word "Image"* (London: Secker & Warburg, 1970), pp. 12–22.

14. See Paul Ricoeur, *The Rule of Metaphor*, trans. Robert Czerny (Toronto: University of Toronto Press, 1977). My debt to this comprehensive survey and analysis of metaphorical language should be apparent to the informed reader, even where I disagree with Ricoeur's conclusions. Without it this paper could not have been written.

15. C. Perelman and L. Olbrechts-Tyteca, *The New Rhetoric: A Treatise on Argumentation* (Notre Dame, Ind.: University of Notre Dame Press, 1969), p. 168.

16. Frances Yates, *The Art of Memory* (Chicago: University of Chicago Press, 1966), pp. 95–96. Also see Furbank, *Reflections*, pp. 108–10.

17. Gaston Bachelard, *L'Air et les songes* (Paris: J. Corti, 1943), p. 10. Trans. Colette Gaudin in Bachelard, *On Poetic Imagination and Reverie* (Indianapolis, Ind.: Bobbs-Merrill, 1971), p. 21.

18. *Rhetoric*, trans. W. Rhys Roberts (New York: Random House, 1954), p. 28.

19. I am following the reasoning of Nicholas Rescher, *A Theory of Possibility* (Oxford: Blackwell, 1975), p. 219: "Though the reality of possibilities resides only in the mind's conception thereof, the critical fact remains that the mind proceeds in this constructive enterprise in a restricted and canalized way, by use of the structured and structuring

framework of a conceptual scheme and the linguistic equipment that gives it concrete embodiment. The realm of the possible is a construct, but the construction is made with the perfectly real materials of the conceptual schemes we use in our description and rationalization of the real world about us."

20. Ernst R. Curtius, *European Literature and the Latin Middle Ages,* trans. W. R. Trask (Princeton, N.J.: Princeton University Press, 1953), pp. 70, 101.

21. Johann Jacob Breitinger, *Critische Dichtkunst* (1740; facsimile reprint ed., Stuttgart: Metzler, 1966), 1 : 61–62.

22. Michel Foucault, *The Order of Things* (New York: Pantheon Books, 1970), p. 357.

23. Edmund Husserl, *Ideas,* trans. W. R. Boyce Gibson (London: Collier, 1962), p. 231.

24. All passages quoted from "Michael" are from *The Poetical Works of William Wordsworth,* 5 vols., ed. Ernest de Selincourt (Oxford: Clarendon Press, 1944), 2 : 80–94.

25. *The Letters of William and Dorothy Wordsworth,* ed. Ernest de Selincourt, 2d ed. rev. C. L. Shaver (Oxford: Clarendon Press, 1967), 1 : 322.

26. The use of these distinctions can be traced back to the discussion by Allen Tate in "Literature As Knowledge" (1941), reprinted in *The Man of Letters in the Modern World* (New York: Meridian Books, 1955), pp. 34– 63. Tate's essay discusses Charles Morris's work on the theory of signs, where these terms were first proposed as an analysis of discursive form.

27. Adam Smith, *An Inquiry into the Nature and Causes of the Wealth of Nations,* ed. J. R. McCulloch (Edinburgh: A. and C. Black, 1863), p. 171.

28. William Wordsworth, "A Letter to the Bishop of Llandaff," *Prose Works,* ed. W. J. B. Owen and J. W. Smyser (Oxford: Clarendon Press, 1974), 1 : 43.

29. C. M. Bouch and G. P. Jones, *A Short Economic and Social History of the Lake Counties* (Manchester: Manchester University Press, 1961), p. 201.

30. Georg Lukács, *The Historical Novel,* trans. H. and S. Mitchell (Harmondsworth: Penguin Books, 1969), p. 116.

31. Bouch and Jones, *History of the Lake Counties,* p. 237.

32. Ibid., p. 218.

33. *Letters,* 1 : 322.

34. Paul Ricoeur, *Freud and Philosophy,* trans. D. Savage (New Haven, Conn.: Yale University Press, 1970), p. 34.

35. Shell's comment on Lessing's "Der Rabe und der Fuchs": "The *Gabe* (gift) turns out to be a *Gift* (poison)," p. 127, n. 38, should have been removed by his readers or editors. This kind of fractured German would suggest to a reader of German that Shell's argument is rather "misty"; such sophomoric bilingual puns are common in first-year language classes, not in a work of scholarship. Heinzelman makes much of Blake's cryptic note: "23 May 1810 found the Word Golden" in his chapter on Blake, but never mentions that Blake uses "golden" and "gold" three times in his annotations on Lavater's *Aphorisms on Man* (1788).

36. See Roman Jakobson's diagram of the communicative process in "Linguistics and Poetics," reprinted in *The Structuralists: From Marx to Lévi-Strauss,* ed. R. T. and F. M. De George (Garden City, N.Y.: Anchor Books, 1972), p. 89.

37. Daniel Stempel, "Blake, Foucault, and the Classical Episteme," *PMLA* 96 (1981): 401.

38. *Instigations of Ezra Pound* (1920; reprint ed., Freeport, Ill.: Books for Libraries Press, 1967), p. 387.

39. Hugh Kenner, *The Pound Era* (Berkeley, Calif.: University of California Press, 1971), p. 230.

40.  The reduction of all structure to visual forms is characteristic of Northrop Frye's criticism, as in *Anatomy of Criticism* (New York: Atheneum, 1967), p. 335: "The link between rhetoric and logic is 'doodle' or associative diagram, the expression of the conceptual by the spatial." But as Wittgenstein points out, not all "pictures" (models) are spatial: "Every picture is *at the same time* a logical one. (On the other hand, not every picture is, for example, a spatial one.)" *Tractatus*, 2.182. Examples of nonspatial links between rhetoric and logic can be found in William Empson's *The Structure of Complex Words* (London: Chatto & Windus, 1953), chap. 2, "Statements in Words," and Käte Hamburger, *The Logic of Literature,* trans. M. J. Rose (Bloomington, Ind.: Indiana University Press, 1973), chap. 2, "Foundations in Theory of Language."

# Notes toward a Marxist Rhetoric

## Robert Wess

### Oregon State University

> . . . there is no error more disabling and actively dangerous to the practice of any human freedom than the notion that there is some "socialist" mode of production . . . which will afford a categorical guarantee that some immanent socialist society (values, ideas, institutions, etc.) will *unfold itself* . . . out of the womb of the mode of production itself. This is wholly untrue: every choice and every institution is still to be made. . . .
>
> —E. P. Thompson

**M**ARXISM is in the midst of a renaissance that bids fair to revise many of the notions commonly thought to constitute the substance of Marxist thought. There are many reasons for this, but a major one is undoubtedly Louis Althusser. In literary theory, his influence has registered itself in varying ways in the innovative work of, among others, Terry Eagleton, Fredric Jameson, and Pierre Macherey. Althusser is also, to put it mildly, a controversial figure. E. P. Thompson has recently confessed that if Althusserianism represents the logical terminus of Marx's thought, he would rather be a Christian— which, I guess, is about the worst thing that one Marxist can say about another.[1]

One reason for the seminality of Althusser's thought is his conception of totality, an important concept for any Marxist. Georg Lukács once even observed: "It is not the primacy of economic motives in historical explanation that constitutes the decisive difference between Marxism and bourgeois thought, but the point of view of totality."[2] Althusser typically presents his conception—we should note his preference for the term *whole* (tout) to *totality* (totalité)[3]—in dialectical opposition to economism, which he persuasively interprets as a misreading of Marx inspired by the Hegelian dialectic. The first major statement of this theme appeared in 1962 in "Contradiction et surdétermination" (Ben Brewster's English translation of this essay appeared in 1969, in *For Marx*); subsequently, the theme has been repeated and refined in a number of places, including one chapter in *Reading Capital*, where the opposition is presented in broad terms in one passage that can serve as our text here:

> We know that the Marxist whole cannot possibly be confused with the Hegelian whole: it is a whole whose unity, far from being the expressive or "spiritual" unity of Leibniz's or Hegel's whole, is constituted by a certain type of *complexity*, the unity of a *structured whole* containing what can be called levels or instances which are distinct and "relatively autonomous," and co-exist within this complex structural unity, articulated with one another according to specific determinations, fixed in the last instance by the level or instance of the economy. [*RC*, p. 97]

By "expressive" unity, Althusser means a unity based on the essence/phenomena distinction in which the inner essence is the sole determinant of the phenomena that embody it. This, according to Althusser, is the core of the Hegelian dialectic, and he contends that it led to a widespread misreading of Marx when the notion that Marx "inverted" Hegel was construed as meaning that he kept Hegel's dialectic intact and simply applied it to a different content, the materiality of economics rather than the spirituality of ideas. So interpreted, the Marxist theory of social formation can be summed up in the familiar notion that the economic "base" is the sole determinant of all "superstructures," which are nothing more than displacements of it that differ only in the degree of the transparency of the displacement.

The influence of this construction of Marx's system of thought on literary theory produced a brand of criticism that is well known. It is easy to see, for example, how the reductionist model of textual analysis—which has long been deplored by those unsympathic to Marxism and stigmatized, by sympathizers whom the model embarrasses, as "vulgar Marxism"—logically follows from the construction, for if ideologies derive directly from the economic base, the interpretation of their textual embodiments is essentially a process of identifying the economic class positions underlying them. Further, the essence of an ideology is located in its specific economic origin, which forever determines its identity on the stage of history. Ideologies are thus essentialized, frozen forever in the image of their origin. Finally, ideologies possess no autonomy whatever. Determined by economic reality, they change as that reality changes in a one to one correspondence—they are nothing more than an epiphenomenal allegory of economic history. Powerless, they are relatively unimportant.

The true Marxist whole, Althusser has argued at length and with great subtlety, is altogether different from the Hegelian-inspired model of economism. It is economistic insofar as the economic level is determinant "in the last instance," but it differs from economism because the economic level is not conceived as the sole determinant of history, the inner essence of all superstructures that are merely its epiphenomena. Rather, the economic level coexists with other levels in a complex interplay of determinations that Althusser identifies with the term "structural causality" (*RC*, p. 186). The key point about "structural causality"—in contrast to "expressive causality," where one independent level causes all the others that express it—is that the ultimate cause is nowhere present as an independent element. The "structural cause" is absent, appearing only in its effects—that is, in the consequences of the interplay among the relatively autonomous levels that constitute the structure. As Fredric Jameson observes, it is this conception of structure that explains "the otherwise incomprehensible prestige and influence of the Althusserian revolution—which has produced powerful and challenging oppositional currents in a host of disciplines, from philosophy proper to political science, anthropology, legal studies, economics, and cultural studies."[4] The seminality of the conception appears most clearly in the notion of "relative autonomy," which implies the possibility of levels that are determin*ed* (their autonomy is only relative) and determin*ing* (they do possess a genuine degree of autonomy).

Fleshing out this abstract conception of the Marxist whole in convincing theoretical detail is obviously an intellectual challenge of the first order. Whether Althusser has met it successfully is questionable, though it would be wrong to say that he has failed altogether. There is, for example, his theory of ideology, the one level or instance in the Althusserian conception of

the Marxist whole that will be examined closely here. Terry
Eagleton, even while faulting this theory, has termed it "ep-
ochal."[5] This is just. For Althusser's work on ideology does
break new ground on which a powerful theory of ideology,
which inevitably will be the collaborative effort of many workers in the area, promises to rise. Further, the rise of such a
theory would clearly be in an area of Marxist thought that has
been underdeveloped in the past. This in itself may be
significant, for one is inclined to attribute the underdevelop-
ment not to mere neglect but to the relative unimportance of
ideology in the tradition of Marxist thought that Althusser has
challenged. If ideology is receiving unprecedented attention
among Marxists today, it is, at least in part, because the Althusserian conception of the Marxist whole gives ideology unprecedented importance. Hence, this essay, even as it departs from
Althusser's position in important ways, will, ironically, be de-
parting from the source that made it possible.

Near the end of "Contradiction and Overdetermination"
Althusser calls for an "elaboration of *the theory of the particular
essence of the specific elements of the superstructure*. Like the map of
Africa before the great explorations, this theory remains a
realm sketched in outline, with its great mountain chains and
rivers, but often unknown in detail beyond a few well-known
regions. Who has *really* attempted to follow up the explorations
of Marx and Engels? I can think only of Gramsci" (*FM*, p. 114).
This is quoted for two reasons: first, the reference to Gramsci—
about which more shortly; second, the italicized reference to
"essence," which attributes a principle of autonomy to superstructural levels such as the ideological. When the project of
this essay was first conceived, two parts were envisioned, the
first circumscribing the theoretical space of the ideological
level, the second filling the space with the essence of the
ideological by adapting for this purpose Kenneth Burke's
classic studies in the field of symbology. But the first part bal-
looned into this full-length essay, so the second is an absence
toward which the conclusion can only point. Further, as the
circumference of the space emerged more clearly, it began to
appear that *rhetoric* rather than *ideology* is the best term for the
essence that it encircles. Hence, there will be throughout the
essay a running critique of the term *ideology*, culminating in a
proposal to substitute for it the term *rhetoric*.

Althusser specifies his indebtedness to Gramsci in "Ideology and Ideological State Apparatuses" when he aligns his theory of the State as a complex of repressive and ideological apparatuses with Gramsci's " 'remarkable' idea that the State could not be reduced to the (Repressive) State Apparatus, but included, as he put it, a certain number of institutions from *'civil society':* the Church, the Schools, the trade unions, etc." (*LP*, p. 142). Accompanying this comment, there is a list of references to discussions of this idea in the *Prison Notebooks*. One of the passages Althusser includes in his list is the following: "What we can do, for the moment, is to fix two major superstructural 'levels': the one that can be called 'civil society,' that is the ensemble of organisms commonly called 'private,' and that of 'political society' or 'the State.' These two levels correspond on the one hand to the function of 'hegemony' which the dominant group exercises throughout society and on the other hand to that of 'direct domination' or command exercised throughout the State and 'juridical' government."[6] This distinction is the same as the idea of "dual perspective" that Gramsci—in a passage Althusser does not include in his list of references—embodies in the famous image of the Machiavellian Centaur: "The dual perspective can present itself on various levels, from the most elementary to the most complex; but these can all theoretically be reduced to two fundamental levels, corresponding to the dual nature of Machiavelli's Centaur—half-animal and half-human. They are the levels of force and of *consent,* authority and hegemony, violence and civilization."[7] The italics are mine and their aim is to emphasize that in Gramsci's treatment of what corresponds to Althusser's ideological state apparatuses a role is given to "consent," which Gramsci elsewhere refers to as "an active and voluntary (free) consent."[8] This disappears in Althusser's theory, and its disappearance is symptomatic of the theory's peculiar tendency to undermine its most seminal features.

The source of this tendency is the presence in the theory of two approaches to ideology that run counter to each other. In one, perhaps best termed the *epistemological,* ideology is opposed to science as falsity to truth. This is, of course, the fashion in which ideology has been most commonly conceived in the Marxist tradition, which synonymized it with the notion of "false consciousness" and gave it the strong pejorative connotations that obscure the new sense the term is acquiring in contemporary critical discourse. An example of the difficulty appears in one of Fredric Jameson's recent essays, where he tells a story of how a discussion of the "ideology of language in Wallace Stevens" was automatically misunderstood as a negative judgment of Stevens. Jameson retorts: "if all ideas and all symbolic forms express group *praxis*, then it is hard to see why saying so should be construed as a blanket repudiation."[9] The new nonpejorative sense of the term derives from an approach to ideology that conceives it as a site of struggle in general and of class struggle in particular. Kenneth Burke's term, *dramatistic*, can serve, at least for the duration of this essay, to distinguish this approach from its competitor in Althusser's theory.

One of the principal achievements of the theory is its conceptualization of the materiality of ideology. The most dramatic consequence of this is Althusser's thesis that ideology is universal:

> *So ideology is as such an organic part of every social totality.* It is as if human societies could not survive without these *specific formations*, these systems of representations (at various levels), their ideologies. Human societies secrete ideology as the very element and atmosphere indispensable to their historical respiration and life. . . . And I am not going to steer clear of the crucial question: *historical materialism cannot conceive that even a communist society could ever do without ideology,* be it ethics, art or "world outlook." [*FM*, p. 232]

Althusser's italics emphasize his radical departure here from earlier Marxist conceptions of ideology. Conceived as "false consciousness," ideology is something that history promises to go beyond. A classic formulation of this view appears in Lukács's theory of class consciousness. As Lukács conceives it, class consciousness is not, of course, to be confused with the ordinary notion of consciousness as subjective immediacy; rather, it is a "possible" consciousness, the rational response that can be "imputed" to a typical position in the process of production. But for nearly every class in history even the fullest realization of the possibilities of consciousness allotted to it by objective economic conditions has not been sufficient to pierce the veil of "false consciousness" that blinds it to the real totality of the productive process. The one exception is the proletariat, historically destined to take the momentous step beyond ideology. The objective conditions of this step are analyzed in detail in "Reification and the Consciousness of the Proletariat," the centerpiece of *History and Class Consciousness*, where the peculiar

oppression that capitalism imposes on the proletariat ironically
turns out to be the enabling condition of its transcendence:

> Above all the worker can only become conscious of his existence in
> society when he becomes aware of himself as a commodity. As we
> have seen, his immediate existence integrates him as a pure, naked
> object into the production process. Once this immediacy turns out
> to be the consequence of a multiplicity of mediations, once it be-
> comes evident how much it presupposes, then the fetishistic forms
> of the commodity system begin to dissolve: in the commodity the
> worker recognizes himself and his own relations with capital. Inas-
> much as he is incapable in practice of raising himself above the role
> of object his consciousness is the *self-consciousness of the commodity;* or
> in other words it is the self-knowledge, the self-revelation of the
> capitalist society founded upon the production and exchange of
> commodities.[10]

Althusser, by universalizing ideology, opens the door to a new
view of it, one in which it appears not as an excretion but as a
determining material power in the process of history.

The most obvious sign of ideology's materiality in Althusser's
theory is in his identification of ideology with concrete social
practices: "an ideology always exists in an apparatus, and its
practice, or practices" (*LP*, p. 166). His list of apparatuses includes the churches, schools, the family, the legal and political
systems, mass media, sports, literature, and the arts. The crucial problem, however, is that of the subject, whose actions constitute the practices inscribed in apparatuses. Whether Althusser successfully solves that problem is dubious, but its clear
formulation is suggested when it is considered in the context of
his conceptualization of the Marxist whole. The problem, in
brief, is that if the ideological instance is to be "relatively autonomous," then the subject must be constituted in the process
of social formation, but in a way that endows it with a constitutive power of its own—it must be determined and determining.

Althusser does part of the job in demonstrating that the ideas
in subjects derive not from a spiritual dimension of the subject
that is prior to sociality but, rather, from the materiality of
concrete social practices. The ideas of the subject are material,
Althusser emphasizes, "in that *his ideas are his material actions
inserted into material practices governed by material rituals which are
themselves defined by the material ideological apparatus from which
derive the ideas of that subject*" (*LP*, p. 169). It is thus in and
through concrete social practices that ideas arise which enable

subjects to identify themselves as subjects—as opposed to mere "individuals," by which Althusser means what Kenneth Burke likes to call, less ambiguously, "bodies"—and to think of themselves as participating willingly in the reproduction of the social practices that generated the ideas in the first place. In this fashion, the subject and its ideas are conceived, not as mere epiphenomena, but as realities that have real effects in the real world. The site of ideology is thus shifted from the epistemological context of true and false consciousness to the dramatistic context of concrete actions and practices.

Althusser's argument here, which is cogent, ironically points to another problem with the term *ideology*, one that crystalizes when Althusser, in listing the consequences of his demonstration of ideology's material existence, announces: "Disappeared: the term *ideas*" (*LP*, p. 169). This suggests that *ideology*, which Destutt de Tracy originally introduced late in the eighteenth century to designate the science of ideas, may have outlived its usefulness, and that it might be better to speak of *symbols* rather than *ideas*. For example, since symbols are inherently social, arising from and acting in social processes, this shift in terminology would eliminate the need for the painstaking argument that Althusser makes to collapse the distinction between a spiritual realm of ideas and a material realm of existence. One could argue, more simply, that symbols are prior to this distinction because, like any other distinction, it is made within the social realm of symbols. Approaching the matter from this angle, one could proceed easily to the question of the historical circumstances of the emergence of the distinction and the specific uses to which it was subsequently put. Furthermore, such a shift in terminology would eliminate the problem that the use of *ideology* now entails because of the pejorative connotations that it acquired after the Marxist tradition took it over.

In "Ideology and Ideological State Apparatuses," Althusser couples his thesis that ideology has a material existence with the thesis that has become the most well-known, a thesis first advanced in "Marxism and Humanism":

> In ideology men do indeed express, not the relation between them and their conditions of existence, but *the way* they live the relation between them and their conditions of existence: this presupposes both a real relation and an *"imaginary," "lived"* relation. Ideology, then, is the expression of the relation between men and their "world," that is, the (overdetermined) unity of the real relation and

the imaginary relation between them and their real conditions of existence. In ideology the real relation is inevitably invested in the imaginary relation, a relation that *expresses* a *will* (conservative, conformist, reformist or revolutionary), a hope or a nostalgia, rather than describing a reality. [*FM*, pp. 233–34]

The term *imaginary* signals the presence of the epistemological approach to ideology that does operate in Althusser's theory. But it would be an error to say that the term is merely a variant of "false consciousness." That would miss the whole significance of his theory. The coupling of "imaginary" with "lived" actually points to the principal aim of the theory, which is to identify ideology with actions that people actually perform in concrete social practices—in other words, to give ideology a material specificity and power in the real world. It is Althusser's materialization of ideology in a multiplicity of social practices that has given this theory its power. Note, for example, Paul Hirst's summation of Althusser's significance:

Ideology has developed a significance and centrality in Marxist theory in the last decade which it had never possessed before. This change represents an attempt to come to terms with pressing political problems and struggles in modern capitalism. The Women's Movement, the struggles around the character and content of education, movements among Blacks and anti-racist struggles, questions of welfare state practices, the political role and effects of the mass media, and so on, have forced Marxists to recognise a complex field of social relations inadequately comprehended by the classic Marxist theories of the economy and politics. Louis Althusser's work is the primary means by which these problems, inadequately signalled under the notion of "ideology," have been thought through in this country [England] and in France.[11]

Still, while the notion of living an imaginary relation to the real clearly points to something important, it does so with a term, *imaginary*, whose presence pushes Althusser's theory toward the outmoded epistemological approach to the ideological, and it is pushed further in that direction by the manner in which Althusser opposes science to ideology. Recall Althusser's distinction between two relations between people and their world, one real and one imaginary—the real relation, of course, is articulated in science. Furthermore, science and ideology are conceived not only as a polar opposition, but also in the absence of any theoretical bridge from one to the other. True, in *Reading Capital*, Althusser recognizes the need for such a bridge

(*RC*, p. 153). But he doesn't provide one there, and the need becomes even more imperative after his correction of the error in that work and in *For Marx*, which he initially called "theoreticism," but now prefers to identify as his "theoreticist deviation" (*ESC*, p. 105). The correction revolves around his famous theory of the "break" between the early and later Marx, his claim, in brief, that the later Marx does not merely revise the earlier writings but actually works within an entirely different problematic. Althusser still insists on the reality of the "break," but admits that he erred in abstracting it from its historical texture and treating it in purely epistemological terms. In his words: "I was led to give a *rationalist* explanation of the 'break,' contrasting *truth* and *error* in the form of the speculative distinction between *science* and *ideology*" (*ESC*, p. 106). Conceived along these lines, the role of ideology in the production of a science would seem to be a negative one, for if ideology is relegated to the abyss of error, it would appear that it could be productive only in the sense that a dialectical antagonist can motivate opposing arguments—for example, one might say that Marx was able to arrive at the true concept of "surplus value" through arguing with the false concept of it articulated by the classical economists. In Althusser's revised version of the "break," which returns it to history, ideology is given a positive role. The "break," Althusser now insists, "refers us to something quite different from a theory of the difference between science and ideology, to something quite different from an epistemology"; it refers us, rather, "to a theory of the material (production), social (division of labor, class struggle), ideological and philosophical conditions of the processes of production of knowledge" (*ESC*, p. 156). But the needed bridge between ideology and science remains, as Alex Callinicos has observed, an absence in Althusser's thought.[12] It's difficult to avoid the suspicion that the motive for such an absence is not theoretical but political.

Althusser's political posture has been, of course, frequently subjected to very severe attack, nowhere more scathingly than in Thompson's "The Poverty of Theory." Callinicos's critique is perhaps worth attending to even more closely than Thompson's total dismissal, however, because Callinicos reads Althusser sympathetically and correctly cites his positive achievements. In this critique, the absence of a bridge between science and ideology is a symptomatic silence, not a mere theoretical loose end: "For the notion that the masses necessarily live in ideology, and that it will therefore be necessary for there to continue to exist a group of those adept in the sciences in order to guide them, derives from this position. Thus conceived, the theory of ideology can serve as a justification for bureaucratic state capitalism in the Eastern bloc."[13] But the question of Althusser's politics is not one that needs to be arbitrated here. The question that does need to be addressed is whether, in view of Althusser's problems with the science/ideology distinction, one should simply discard it altogether. That move is tempting and may be the right one, but before making it perhaps it would be worthwhile to try, experimentally, to relate science and ideology in a manner that is consistent with the dramatistic approach to ideology. The proposal to be developed here is to view the relationship as a paradoxical one in which ideology is both the container of science and contained by it.

Jameson's recent work on ideology, which he calls "a practical exploration of Althusser's seminal definition of the ideological," suggests a fruitful way of beginning.[14] For Jameson subtly transforms the theory when he takes the concept of the "imaginary," which in Althusser ambiguously straddles the abstract realm of epistemology and the concrete realm of symbolic practices, and puts it unambiguously into the second of these realms as he argues that ideology is "necessarily narrative in its structure, inasmuch as it not only involves a mapping of the real, but also the essentially narrative or fantasy attempt of the subject to invent a place for himself/herself in a collective and historical process which excludes him or her and which is itself basically nonrepresentable and non-narrative."[15] "The narrative apparatus which informs ideological representations is thus," Jameson concludes, "not mere 'false consciousness,' but an authentic way of grappling with a Real that must always transcend it, a Real into which the subject seeks to insert itself through praxis, all the while painfully learning the lesson of its own ideological closure and of history's resistance to the fantasy-structures in which it is itself locked."[16] This conceptualization of ideology, published in 1979, should be read in the context of the theoretical space Jameson charts brilliantly in "Marxism and Historicism," published the same year, where he demonstrates the thesis that our only access to history, which itself is not a narrative, is through narrative and offers us a narrative paradigm within which to place ourselves in the contemporary situation, a paradigm summed up in the essay's closing lines as "a hermeneutic relationship to the past which is able to grasp its own present as history only on condition it manages to keep the idea of the future, and of radical and Utopian transformation, alive."[17]

Perhaps the most significant moment in the essay occurs when Jameson denies any "place of truth" outside the discursive realm of narrative in which we all necessarily live, a place that science characteristically claims for itself and that Althusser, despite his correction of his early "theoreticist deviation," refuses to relinquish. Jameson identifies his position here as "an absolute Marxist historicism" and explicitly marks it as a departure from Althusserian doctrine.[18] While this does, as Jameson notes, relativize science, it does not necessarily subjectivize it. This latter point is not one that he theorizes, but he does cite an example in Marx to illustrate the "scandalous" notion that absolute scientific truth can have, as its enabling condition, historical contingencies. Yet, upon reflection, there is perhaps more common sense than scandal in the notion. For unless one wants to attribute the demand for objectivity and the elaborate procedures that sciences have devised to guarantee it to divine intervention in human affairs, one must look for the motivation of these concrete practices in the materiality of history, in the needs of men and women living and acting in the real world. Put in terms of Jameson's conceptualization of ideology, people devising strategies for action within the framework of the narrative that informs their living will necessarily encounter the need for the best information they can muster about the Real. Stated axiomatically, any narrative carves out a space for a science.

In the case of Jameson's revolutionary narrative, the science would appear to arise in the space marked off by the category he calls "cultural revolution," since he suggests that "this new unifying category of historical study" is "the only one in terms of which the so-called human sciences can be reorganized in a properly materialistic way."[19] Jameson proposes this category in the context of a discussion of the Althusserian concept of "mode of production" and the discussion suggests, in broad outline, the direction in which his proposed materialistic reorganization of the human sciences might go. For he argues that no mode of production (feudal, capitalist, etc.) exists in a pure state; rather any social formation is both a sedimentation of past modes of production and anticipatory of future modes. It is this that leads him to propose "cultural revolution" as an englobing category in place of "mode of production." And this leads, in turn, to the proposition that the principle of cultural revolution has, throughout history, been articulated in quite different structural embodiments. While Jameson doesn't say so explicitly, the proposition is clearly directed against the traditional economistic model of transformation, which dictated that the gun of revolutionary change can only be loaded in the economic infrastructure. Nonetheless, there would still seem to be one general first principle for this new science of cultural revolution, a principle entailed in Jameson's view that the narrative principle informing ideology grapples with a Real that always transcends it. In brief, the fundamental error that one must vigilantly resist is to mistake one's narrative for history itself. Consequently, while the science is contained within the narrative that creates a need for it, the science points beyond the narrative to the Real that contains it.

It is here that one can properly invoke Althusser's theoretical antihumanism. Of all the dimensions of Althusser's work, this is surely the prime cause of its notoriety in many circles, especially in those that choose to scoff at the notion of "antihumanism" without seriously considering the significance of the qualifier, "theoretical." For what Althusser attacks in the name of antihumanism is a way of theorizing history that is becoming increasingly untenable even while continuing to have a firm place in the commonplaces of everyday discourse: "Marx's theoretical anti-humanism, as it operates within historical materialism, thus means a refusal to root the explanation of social formations and their history in a concept of man with theoretical pretensions, that is, a concept of man as an *originating subject,* one in whom originate his needs *(homo oeconomicus),* his thoughts *(homo rationalis),* and his acts and struggles *(homo moralis, juridicus* and *politicus)*" *(ESC,* p. 205). Perhaps the easiest way to get Althusser's point is to recall the famous passage at the beginning of Marx's *18th Brumaire:* "Men make their own history, but they do not make it just as they please; they do not make it under circumstances chosen by themselves, but under circumstances directly encountered, given and transmitted from the past." Althusser's contention is that theoretical humanism mistakenly abridges the statement to read merely: "Men make their own history." And this is a mistake that narrative obviously fosters because of its inducements to think in terms of human origins and destinies.

Althusser's admonitions against theoretical humanism thus merit attention. But in attending to them, one soon encounters the problem of deciding whether Althusser, in placing himself polemically in opposition to the tradition of humanist history, ends up going to the opposite extreme and erasing altogether Marx's "men make their own history." Althusser has, of course, often been criticized for doing precisely this. Thompson's "The Poverty of Theory" is the most notable example; there, for nearly two hundred pages, Thompson pummels Althusser from one page to the next for (1) limiting the role of human subjects in history to that of bearing structures within architectonic modes of production and (2) conceiving the architectonic structures, finally, in idealist terms. Althusser's own sensitivity to such criticism surfaces in a curious way in *Essays in Self-Criticism* as he reviews and responds to the controversies that his earlier work spawned. For there he seeks to deflect the criticism from his reading of Marx to capitalism: "It is very important to understand why Marx considers men in this case only as 'supports' of a relation, or 'bearers' of a function in the production process, determined by the production relation. It is not at all because he reduces men in their concrete life to simple bearers of functions: he considers them as such in this respect because the capitalist production relation reduces them to this simple function within the infrastructure, in production, that is, in exploitation" (*ESC*, p. 202).

Althusser's theoretical antihumanism should thus serve as a reminder of two key problems: (1) the need to place the subject inside the Real that contains it and (2) the danger, in doing this, of dissolving the subject into a mere function of the Real in a manner that denies it any genuine autonomy. The first of these problems is effectively solved in Althusser's thesis on the materiality of ideology, for this thesis argues that the subject is constituted in ideology, and this argument, by demonstrating that the subject is posterior to the social formation, is simultaneously an argument against the humanist ontologizing of the subject as the origin and destiny of history. The second problem remains—how can a subject that is posterior to the social formation possess any genuine autonomy within it?

In "Ideology and Ideological State Apparatuses," Althusser begins with the thesis that "the ultimate condition of produc-

tion is . . . the reproduction of the conditions of production"
(*LP*, p. 127). This first step is crucial because it is the way that he
chooses to nail down ideology, and the constitution of the subject within it, in the materiality of history. The essay then proceeds by positioning ideology within the overall process of reproduction and, finally, by constituting the subject within the
operations of the various ideological state apparatuses. What
results is a subject conceived purely as an instrument whose
purpose is dictated by the mode of production that shapes it in
accordance with what it needs to reproduce itself:

> Each mass ejected *en route* is practically provided with the ideology
> which suits the role it has to fulfil in class society: the role of the
> exploited (with a "highly-developed" "professional," "ethical,"
> "civic," "national" and a-political consciousness); the role of the
> agent of exploitation (ability to give the workers orders and speak
> to them: "human relations"), of the agent of repression (ability to
> give orders and enforce obedience "without discussion," or ability
> to manipulate the demagogy of a political leader's rhetoric), or of
> the professional ideologist (ability to treat consciousnesses with the
> respect, i.e., with the contempt, blackmail, and demagogy they de-
> serve, adapted to the accents of Morality, of Virtue, of "Transcen-
> ence," of the Nation, of France's World Role, etc.). [*LP*, pp. 155–
> 56]

Note that even the exploiters are located within ideology. Consistent with his theory that ideology is an organic condition of
living in a social formation, Althusser insists that "the ruling
class does not maintain with the ruling ideology, which is its
own ideology, an external and lucid relation of pure utility and
cunning. . . . In reality, the bourgeoisie has to believe in its own
myth before it can convince others . . . since what it lives in its
ideology is *the very relation* between it and its real conditions of
existence which allows it simultaneously to act on itself . . . and
on others . . . so as to take up, occupy and maintain its historical
role as a ruling class" (*FM*, p. 234).

A curious feature of "Ideology and Ideological State Apparatuses" is its closing section, where Althusser offers a concrete illustration and chooses for his example of ideology the
Christian religion. The justification offered is reasonable
enough—the essay presents a theory of the formal structure of
all ideology, a structure conceived as "omnipresent, trans-
historical and therefore immutable in form throughout the extent of history" (*LP*, p. 161), so any concrete example can,

theoretically, illustrate the universal formal structure as well as any other. But the choice of this particular example remains curious because, earlier in the essay, Althusser argued that in the modern era the School has replaced the Church as the dominant ideological state apparatus. The choice one suspects is not arbitrary, especially when one considers the essay's explicit equation of subjecthood to subjection and thinks of how the authoritarian structure of Christianity facilitates the illustration of this in concrete terms.

Christianity provides Althusser with the fundamental distinction that he needs between Subject and subjects—God and selves modeled in his image. This distinction is employed within a subject/object problematic in which the constitution of the subject is conceived as a moment of "recognition" of one's subjecthood in him. The moment of constitution is thus identified as a moment of willing obedience: "the individual *is interpellated as a (free) subject in order that he shall submit freely to the commandments of the Subject, i.e., in order that he shall (freely) accept his subjection,* i.e., in order that he shall make the gestures and actions of his subjection 'all by himself.' *There are no subjects except by and for their subjection.* That is why they 'work all by themselves'" (*LP*, p. 182). Here, more than anywhere else, one feels mired deep within the economistic model that Althusser, elsewhere, promises to lead us out of. What is a subject that exists by and for its subjection if not a robot that is nothing more than an epiphenomenon of the mode of production that produced it?

To Althusser's credit there is the brief postscript to "Ideology and Ideological State Apparatuses" that he added a year after completing the essay. There, he criticizes the essay in observing that to view ideology from the standpoint of reproduction is perhaps too "abstract" and proposes to view it, instead, from the standpoint of the class struggle. The recognition of the need for this correction, one surmises, occurred as Althusser revised his conceptualization of the "break" in Marx's development, for that revision led him to explain the emergence of the science of history in Marx's mind as a consequence of his engagement in political and ideological class struggle. Althusser even argues, in "On the Evolution of the Young Marx," that Marx's adoption of a proletarian class position was a necessary condition of the founding of the science of history because it is only from this standpoint that the exploitative mechanisms of class society become "visible" (*ESC,* p. 161). The problem, obviously, is that it's impossible to explain the formation of a subject, like Marx, actively engaged in opposition to the bourgeois order of his day, in terms of a theory in which the subject exists by and for its subjection. A radically different theory is clearly needed. The postscript thus deconstructs much of "Ideology and Ideological State Apparatuses."

The revisions needed in the theory of ideology appear obliquely in another part of Althusser's system of thought, namely, in his new conception of philosophy. In the early work—*For Marx* and *Reading Capital*—philosophy was virtually assimilated to science: on the one hand, there were specific scientific practices; on the other, there was philosophy, the general theory of theoretical practice—generalities I, II, and III—that has since become well known. But in correcting the early work, he radically altered his view of the relationship between science and philosophy; the major statement of the altered view is "Lenin and Philosophy" (*LP,* pp. 23–70). Science remains in a peculiarly subjectless realm that floats above history, but philosophy is brought down from the sky, identified as the class struggle on the level of theory, and assigned the task of protecting science from the perennial threat of idealism. Hence, in *Essays in Self-Criticism,* as Althusser retrospectively reviews this revision in his thought, he finds it convenient to draw on the image of a battlefield to characterize philosophy: "A philosophy does not make its appearance in the world as Minerva appeared to the society of Gods and men. It only exists in so far as it occupies a position, and it only occupies this position in so far as it has conquered it in the thick of an already occupied world" (*ESC,* p. 165). The only problem with the battlefield image is that it overemphasizes division at the expense of identification, thus deflecting attention away from the way that any division in a battle is simultaneously an alignment with one's allies. But properly discounted, the image of the battlefield suggests an appropriate model for the constitution of the subject in a social formation: it is a process informed by multiple alignments and divisions.

Such a subject is clearly not the centered subject of theoretical humanism. This undoubtedly would meet with the approval of contemporary deconstructionist theorists, who seem paradoxically both to lament and to celebrate our decentered state. But such a subject is not *necessarily* decentered either. For the historicizing of the formation of the subject, instead of ontologizing away the possibility of a centered subject, leaves the question open to history. Whether a centered subject is possible becomes a question of whether historical conditions force contradictions to arise among the multiple alignments and divisions that constitute the subject or make possible a harmonious interplay. Hence, at the very least, a centered subject can be placed in the Utopian future that culminates Jameson's narrative paradigm.[20]

Of the various historical conditions that work for or against a centered subject, the class struggle is obviously of central importance. But whether one wants to remain solidly within the Marxist tradition and place all one's eggs in this basket is another question. When Althusser observes "it is only from the point of view of the classes, i.e., of the class struggle, that it is possible to explain the ideolog*ies* existing in a social formation" (*LP,* p. 185), he takes a firm step beyond his original theory of ideology, but it is not a very big step. For it is clear that he has in mind only two ideologies, bourgeois and proletarian. It is quite likely that he would concede that various ideological state apparatuses all have relatively distinct ideologies, but it is equally clear that he would insist that one could detect in each of them the class position it expresses. Thinking along these lines is fatal because, in doing so, one assumes (1) that ideology is a representation and (2) that it is a representation shaped by a preexistent and economistically grounded subject/object relationship. The difficulties this entails appear strikingly in attempts to derive racist and sexist ideologies from the capitalist mode of production. It is clear that these ideologies have been employed oppressively in the capitalist system of exploitation, but to derive them from this system is a very different and very dubious matter. In short, it is doubtful that all the alignments and divisions involved in the process of subject formation can be reduced to purely economic terms.

To take the big step that Althusser refuses, one must reject altogether the subject/object problematic. Althusser has, of course, rejected this problematic on the level of science, where he has substituted for it the problematic of signification and conceived of knowledge, in opposition to both empiricism and idealism, as a concrete practice in discourse. But Althusser retains the subject/object problematic on the ideological level, thus freezing ideology forever in the categories of a discourse that has an identifiable history. Hirst has argued convincingly, furthermore, that the retention of this problematic decon-structs Althusser's project to remove ideology from the realm of consciousness to the materiality of concrete social practice, because in the "recognition" mechanism by which Althusser constitutes the subject there are subjective attributes, silently presupposed, that preexist the social formation and are the enabling condition of the "recognition" that signals the entry into it.[21] Within the problematic of signification, on the other hand, the subject is constituted in the field of signifying prac-tices involved in the multiple alignments and divisions charac-teristic of any complex social formation. Entry into the field and self-definition within it presuppose nothing more than the irrefutable fact that human beings master symbol systems. There is definitely no need to presuppose anything resembling traditional categories of the subject, such as "will," "desire," and "reason," since these are all denied ontological status. Their presence in or absence from any social field of symbolic significations is an event in history.

The transference of the problem of ideology to the problem-atic of signification entails a radical transformation in custom-ary habits of thought. Instead of thinking of ideology as a rep-resentation that reflects its origin, one must begin thinking of it as a symbolic action with persuasive power in concrete social and economic situations. This essay is conceived as pointing toward a Marxist rhetoric precisely because the term *rhetoric* facilitates this transformation. The fundamental fact that the problematic of signification enables one to conceptualize clearly is that even when a signifying practice has an identifiable class origin, it does not always and forever necessarily serve that class. It can, conceivably, even end up being used against the interests of the class that originated it. In the war of signifying practices, cooptation is always an available strategy. The ulti-mate implication of this appears in Hirst's claim that "no 'ideological' form or social relation is in essence and in principle bourgeois or nonbourgeois."[22] Whether this is equally true in every case is a difficult question that it is perhaps wise not to try to answer in advance. But it clearly is true in some cases. The rhetoric of the feminist movement, for example, has inspired both radicalism and reformism. It is precisely this that makes the movement a site of struggle in the contemporary social formation.

The subject, then, is a signifying practice—or, more precisely, a conjunction of signifying practices—and the relative autonomy of the subject is a function of the relative autonomy of the field of signification from prior material determinations. The placement of the subject in this field necessitates dealing with the difficulty that literary texts, which subjects produce, are also conjunctions of signifying practices. The problem of the relation between subjects and texts, both constituted within the same field of signification, is one that a Marxist rhetoric would have to address. Though one can imagine trying to deny an essential difference between subject and text, it seems likely that it would be more fruitful to distinguish between them, while recognizing that they may be closely related in complex ways. That is the line of inquiry which Althusser points toward in his "Letter on Art," where he suggestively distinguishes between "ideology" as the subject's experience of living and "art" as a distinctive practice that arises from ideology, but detaches itself from its parent and thereby illuminates it (*LP*, pp. 221–27).

Any solution to the subject/text problem depends, however, on a successful solution to a prior problem. For a Marxist rhetoric depends not only on the autonomy of the field of signification, but also on the relativity of that autonomy—in other words, it's essential to resist the temptation to conceptualize the field as totally autonomous. That temptation is, of course, inevitable within the problematic of signification. The popularity, first, of structuralism and, now, of deconstruction is a sign that most academic intellectuals who step into the theoretical space of this problematic are drawn there by the mirage of a totally autonomous language. This is a dead end. The autonomy of language conceptualized in deconstruction is a labyrinth of textual mechanisms that one can enter only at the price of surrendering the power to say anything about anything, including, ironically, language itself.[23] One wonders if the textual machine of deconstruction is best viewed as a curious inverted mirror image of economism. In any case, both clearly erase us and refuse us any power to act in the world. In the context of contemporary critical discourse, the first essen-

tial task of a Marxist rhetoric is thus to secure the relative autonomy of signification in opposition to the challenge of deconstruction.

The autonomy of the rhetorical field of signification resides
in the real consequences it has in the real world. This autonomy
is relative because material circumstances independent of the
field limit its power in significant ways. We can still say, for
example, that the class struggle is determinant "in the last instance," though only in the sense that in the long run of history
it matters very much who wins.[24] Further, in the short run of
the present and the immediate future, the state of the struggle
plays a crucial role in determining the power any signifying
practice exercises. And subjects, in constituting and reconstitut-
ing themselves in the rhetorical field, often do so in ways that
serve primarily their material interests; that is an insight of
traditional ideological analysis that it's obviously important not
to lose. But such material factors, while important, are not all-
important. Persuasion is not a mere reflex of economic class
position. Even Althusser, in a passage quoted earlier, points to,
without actually identifying, a level of persuasion beyond strict
economic materiality when he insists that "the ruling class does
not maintain with the ruling ideology, which is its own ideology,
an external and lucid relation of pure utility and cunning. . . .
In reality, the bourgeoisie has to believe in its own myth before
it can . . . act on itself . . . and on others . . . so as to take up,
occupy and maintain its historical role as a ruling class." This
level of persuasion is precisely the one that Kenneth Burke
identifies, at the outset of *A Rhetoric of Motives,* as the principal
object of his inquiry:

> But besides this job of reclamation, we also seek to develop our
> subject beyond the traditional bounds of rhetoric. There is an in-
> termediate area of expression that is not wholly deliberate, yet not
> wholly unconscious. It lies midway between aimless utterance and
> speech directly purposive. For instance, a man who identifies his
> private ambitions with the good of the community may be partly
> justified, partly unjustified. He may be using a mere pretext to gain
> individual advantage at the public expense; yet he may be quite
> sincere, or even may willingly make sacrifices in behalf of such
> identification. Here is a rhetorical area not analyzable either as
> sheer design or as sheer simplicity. And we would treat of it here.[25]

Charting the range of this level of persuasion and the sources
of its power is the special task of a much-needed Marxist
rhetoric.

# Notes

1. E. P. Thompson, *The Poverty of Theory and Other Essays* (New York: Monthly Review Press, 1978), p. 189.

2. Georg Lukács, *History and Class Consciousness,* trans. Rodney Livingstone (Cambridge, Mass.: MIT Press, 1971), p. 27.

3. Louis Althusser, "Est-il simple d'être Marxiste en philosophie?", *La Pensée,* October 1975, p. 14; an English translation of this passage appears in *Essays in Self-Criticism,* trans. Grahame Lock (London: NLB, 1976), p. 181. All subsequent references to Althusser will be included in the text; the abbreviations used are the following: *ESC—Essays in Self-Criticism; FM—For Marx,* trans. Ben Brewster (New York: Pantheon Books, 1969); *LP—Lenin and Philosophy and Other Essays,* trans. Ben Brewster (New York: Monthly Review Press, 1971); *RC—Reading Capital,* trans. Ben Brewster (London: NLB, 1970).

4. Fredric Jameson, *The Political Unconscious: Narrative as a Socially Symbolic Act* (Ithaca, N.Y.: Cornell University Press, 1981), p. 37.

5. Terry Eagleton, "Ideology, Fiction, Narrative," *Social Text* 2 (1979): 62.

6. Antonio Gramsci, *Selections from the Prison Notebooks of Antonio Gramsci,* ed. and trans. Quintin Hoare and Geoffrey Nowell Smith (New York: International Publishers, 1971), p. 12.

7. Ibid., pp. 169–70.

8. Ibid., p. 271.

9. Fredric Jameson, "Ideology and Symbolic Action," *Critical Inquiry* 5 (1978): 419.

10. Lukács, *History and Class Consciousness,* p. 168.

11. Paul Hirst, *On Law and Ideology* (Atlantic Highlands, N.J.: Humanities Press, 1979), p. 1.

12. Alex Callinicos, *Althusser's Marxism* (London: Pluto Press, 1976), p. 62. Callinicos notes elsewhere (p. 85) that there are "intimations" of the needed bridge, but they are nothing more than that.

13. Ibid., p. 101.

14. Fredric Jameson, *Fables of Aggression: Wyndham Lewis, the Modernist as Fascist* (Berkeley: University of California Press, 1979), p. 12.

15. Ibid.

16. Ibid., p. 13.

17. Fredric Jameson, "Marxism and Historicism," *New Literary History* 11 (1979): 72.

18. Ibid., p. 58.

19. Ibid., p. 69.

20. Compare Jameson's "Imaginary and Symbolic in Lacan: Marxism, Psychoanalytic Criticism, and the Problem of the Subject," *Yale French Studies,* No. 55/56 (1977), pp. 338–95, where Jameson approaches the problem of the subject from a different direction, but concludes with a similar proposal: "The solution can only lie, it seems to me, in the renewal of Utopian thinking, of creative speculation as to the place of the subject at the other end of historical time, in a social order which has put behind it class organization, commodity production and the market, alienated labor, and the implacable determinism of an historical logic beyond the control of humanity. Only thus can a third term be imagined beyond either the 'autonomous individualism' of the bourgeoisie in its heyday or the schizoid part-objects in which the fetishization of the subject under late capitalism has left its trace; a term in the light of which both of these forms of consciousness can be placed in their proper historical perspective" (p. 393).

21. Hirst, *On Law and Ideology,* pp. 64–68.

22. Ibid., p. 55.

23. I'm thinking here particularly of the work of Paul de Man, who has pursued the implications of deconstruction with remarkable rigor, even to the ultimate point of systematically turning the deconstructionist theory of textuality on itself. In "The Resistance to Theory," *Yale French Studies*, No. 63 (1982), pp. 3–20, de Man observes that "we seem to assume all too readily that, when we refer to something called 'language,' we know what it is we are talking about, although there is probably no word to be found in the language that is as overdetermined, self-evasive, disfigured and disfiguring as 'language'" (p. 13); and he concludes:

> Technically correct rhetorical readings may be boring, monotonous, predictable and unpleasant, but they are irrefutable. They are also totalizing (and potentially totalitarian) for since the structures and functions they expose do not lead to the knowledge of an entity (such as language) but are an unreliable process of knowledge production that prevents all entities, including linguistic entities, from coming into discourse as such, they are indeed universals, consistently defective models of language's impossibility to be a model language. . . . They are theory and not theory at the same time, the universal theory of the impossibility of theory. [P. 20]

De Man's linguistic skepticism receives its most thorough articulation in *Allegories of Reading* (New Haven, Conn.: Yale University Press, 1979), especially in the demonstration of its central claim that "the allegory of reading narrates the impossibility of reading" (p. 77).

It's difficult (and foolish) not to sympathize with de Man in *Blindness and Insight* (New York: Oxford University Press, 1971) as he points to the pathos of Husserl, in the thirties, never questioning "the privileged viewpoint of the post-Hellenic, European consciousness" precisely "at the moment when Europe was about to destroy itself as center in the name of its unwarranted claim to be the center" (p. 16). But one wonders if de Man, in his resolve to pay whatever intellectual price is necessary to avoid such pathos, has involved himself unwittingly (?) in a species of very high comedy. Recall Derrida's answer to a question (Jean Hyppolite's) raised in response to "Structure, Sign, and Play in the Discourse of the Human Sciences," his well-known contribution to *The Structuralist Controversy: The Languages of Criticism and the Sciences of Man*, ed. Richard Macksey and Eugenio Donato (Baltimore, Md.: The Johns Hopkins University Press, 1972): "I was wondering myself if I know where I am going. So I would answer you by saying, first, that I am trying, precisely, to put myself at a point so that I do not know any longer where I am going" (p. 267). This wry remark, it has always seemed to me, displays dramatically both the value of deconstruction as a medicine we should all take occasionally and the ultimate futility of becoming addicted to it.

24. This use of Althusser's phrase "in the last instance" is, of course, not Althusserian; my point is that history is more like a drama than an object of scientific knowledge. But it should be noted that in the wake of Althusser's antihistoricism the primary object of scientific knowledge among Marxist theorists has tended to become the synchrony of a mode of production rather than the diachrony of history.

25. Kenneth Burke, *A Rhetoric of Motives* (New York: Prentice-Hall, 1950), pp. xiii–xiv.

# *Literature, Rhetoric, Interpretation*

# The Power of Nothing in *Women in Love*

## Daniel O'Hara

### Temple University

"It's the old story—action and reaction, and nothing between."
—D. H. Lawrence

## I

THE question most insistently raised by recent literary criticism is the status and authority of the critic's own voice. Declaring that the idea of the self is a demonstrable fiction puts radically into question the critic who asserts this position. Of course, one strategy for avoiding this dilemma is the claim that the very rigor of the discourse that deconstructs the self recuperates the idea of the self on the metacritical level. Paul de Man has expressed this view most succinctly:

> Within the epistemological labyrinth of figural structures [in a critic's text], the recuperation of selfhood would be accomplished by the rigor with which the discourse deconstructs the very notion of the self. The originator of this discourse is then no longer the dupe of his own wishes; he is as far beyond pleasure and pain as he is beyond good and evil or, for that matter, beyond strength and weakness. His consciousness is neither happy nor unhappy, nor does he possess any power. He remains however a center of authority to the extent that the very destructiveness of his ascetic reading testifies to the validity of his interpretation.[1]

De Man, naturally, does not subscribe to this point of view. He asserts that no critic can master his discourse and no critic's discourse can achieve the kind of invulnerability to the ceaseless ironic reversals of language assumed by this position, not even the discourse that repeatedly enunciates this very principle:

> The discourse by which the figural structure of the self is asserted
> fails to escape from the categories it claims to deconstruct, and this
> remains true, of course, of any discourse which pretends to re-
> inscribe in its turn the figure of this aporia. There can be no escape
> from the dialectical movement of the text.[2]

The critic who would expose the dreaded hand of the onto-
theological tradition under every privileged figure in another's
text should look first to the figures of his own text. And the
metacritic who makes this assertion can never escape either the
tradition he would subvert or the destructive discourse he has
put into play. The dialectical movement of the text that de Man
refers to here is, needless to say, a continuously arrested
dialectic generated by the interplay of its grammatical structures, rhetorical figures, and logical maneuvers. There can be
no final synthetic resolution:

> nothing, whether deed, word, thought or text, ever happens in
> relation, positive or negative, to anything that precedes, follows or
> exists elsewhere, but only as a random event whose power, like the
> power of death, is due to the randomness of its occurrence.[3]

The power of this nothing is what I wish to explore in Lawrence's *Women in Love*.

But first I want to raise another question: of what use is a
critical position that reduces the writing of a text to the blind
attempt of the critic to kiss a shattered mirror whole? For one
thing, it helps to account for some of the stranger spectacles in
recent criticism. A critic as sophisticated as Paul de Man, who
knows the truth of deconstruction, would build into his own
discourse the elements of a parodic reduction of his position.
Such a critic would thereby enact the ironic, arrested dialectic
of textual production that at every moment threatens to explode the critical project into convulsions of mockery. How else
account for Harold Bloom's embrace of the Gnostic Sophia he
previously scorned, or Edward W. Said's apparent obsession
with Flaubert's Egyptian concubine, or Jacques Derrida's fascination with Nietzsche's misplaced umbrella?[4] To secure temporarily their critical authority from the threat of the aporia
described by de Man these critics practice a radical form of
modernist irony that places in the hands of the reader preliminary sketches for a parodic interpretation of the critic even as
such irony protects the articulation of the critic's overall position. Like the great modernist masters of irony, Joyce, Mann,

Valéry, or Lawrence, contemporary critics create in their texts ironic portraits of the authors of these texts. The principle is to do unto oneself before the text itself does one in.

This brings us to a second use of de Man's position, as well as to an example of de Man's own complex irony at work on himself. In his reading of an incident from Rousseau's *Confessions*, de Man, in a playful spirit, takes seriously Rousseau's attempt to excuse himself for accusing a servant girl, Marion, of the theft of a ribbon, which he himself had committed. De Man argues that when Rousseau asserts that he is innocent of blame, that he is not responsible because he had merely excused himself "upon the first thing that offered itself," he is speaking correctly. For the linguistic machine has operated impersonally to produce from the play of signifiers the proper sonorous designation at hand, "Marion."[5] And in a scene from the *Fourth Rêverie* this machine has replicated its own figure and has dramatized the precarious position of the writer in relation to the seductive processes of textual production:

> "I looked at the metal rolls, my eyes were attracted by their polish. I was tempted to touch them with my fingers and I moved them with pleasure over the polished surface of the cylinder."[6]

What staging of the critic's desire could be clearer than this scene?

De Man is arguing for the fundamental impersonality, anonymity, and arbitrariness of discursive practices. A kind of Kantian unconscious, a spontaneous play of linguistic and grammatical structures, or rhetorical tropes and metaphorical conceptions, interrupts and subverts the action of human intentionality. De Man announces this position, however, not with lamentation but with a kind of bewildering joy, a delightful freedom from any responsibility for one's utterances, an irresponsibility that explains the attractiveness of deconstruction and, as well, functions as the basis for any future critiques of the deconstructive enterprise. De Man names this curious freedom in which one self-consciously identifies with the agency of one's own enslavement and so anticipates all possible criticism: "irony."

> Irony is no longer a trope but the undoing of the deconstructive allegory of all tropological cognitions, the systematic undoing, in other words, of understanding. As such, far from closing off the tropological system, irony enforces the repetition of its aberration.[7]

The critic, no matter how aware, is condemned to this kind of freedom—the freedom of irony.

Different critics give different names to this systematic undoing of understanding. Bloom calls it "influence," Lacan calls it "the discourse of the Other," or the "Unconscious," and Derrida calls it by various nondenominational names, but most consistently "différance." Each of these "terms" functions for these critics as irony does for de Man here—a term I think is perhaps the most comprehensive. These master "nonterms" allow the critic to perform any operation upon a text and it is all acceptable because his arguments have built into them the assumption of their own ultimate meaninglessness. Whereas critics and thinkers in the literary and philosophical traditions propounded concepts they asserted were univocal, stable, and pristine, contemporary theoreticians of deconstruction articulate sets of terms that are just the opposite: polyvalent, corrosive, and messy. Reading contemporary criticism is often like watching someone pirouette between the horns of a stuffed bull: all the simulation of meaning, but none of the actual risk.

Even as apparently "relevant" a thinker as Michel Foucault is not immune from the seductions of his own irony. For example, in his introductory volume of *The History of Sexuality* Foucault places Lawrence as a representative of that modern effort to get sex to talk that is the peculiar form of the modern will to knowledge.

According to Foucault we delight now in the pleasure that arises from our power to make the supposedly unspeakable tell all:

> The medical examination, the psychiatric investigation, the pedagogical report, and family controls . . . function as mechanisms with a double impetus: pleasure and power. The pleasure that comes of exercising a power that questions, monitors, watches, spies, searches out, palpates, brings to light; and on the other hand, the pleasure that kindles at having to evade this power, flee from it, fool it, or travesty it. The power that lets itself be invaded by the pleasure it is pursuing. And opposite it, power asserting itself in the pleasure of showing off, scandalizing or resisting. Capture and seduction, confrontation and mutual reinforcement: parents and children, adults and adolescents, educators and students, doctors and patients, the psychiatrist with his hysteric and his perverts, all have played this game continually since the nineteenth century. These attractions, these evasions, these circular incitements have traced around bodies and sexes, not boundaries not to be crossed, but *perpetual spirals of power and pleasure.*[8]

And Lawrence, according to Foucault, participates in this complex round of pleasure-knowledge-power that makes up the history of sexuality in the West from the end of the eighteenth century to the present.

Foucault at the conclusion of his little book quotes two statements from Lawrence—one from *The Plumed Serpent* and the other from *Psychoanalysis and the Unconscious*—to show how Lawrence, as a major literary inventor of the discourse of human sexuality, seeks both to evade that discourse by making sex sacred and unnameable and to propose the fullest articulation yet of the thought of sex:

> "It is sex," said Kate in *The Plumed Serpent.* "How wonderful sex can be, when men keep it powerful and sacred, and it fills the world! like sunshine through and through one!"

> "There has been so much action in the past," said D. H. Lawrence, "especially sexual action, a wearying repetition over and over, without a corresponding thought, a corresponding realization. Now our business is to realize sex. Today the full conscious realization of sex is even more important than the act itself."[9]

In other words, Lawrence is just an instance, a convenient illustration, of Foucault's hypothesis.

Foucault is able to assimilate Lawrence (among others) to his critical project because he, too, possesses a master "nonterm," *discourse*, which allows Foucault to proceed even as it implicates him to some extent in the critique he mounts against the Western "will-to-knowledge." Lawrence's work in his time, like Foucault's in our own, is the manifestation of a particular complex set of rules for the formation of texts on the subject of human sexuality. That is, Lawrence is a locus for the complex network of discursive practices dealing with the topic:

> one is dealing with mobile and transitory points of resistance, producing cleavages in a society that shift about, fracturing unities and effecting regroupings, furrowing across individuals themselves, cutting them up and remolding them, marking off irreducible regions in them, in their bodies and minds. Just as the network of power relations ends by forming a dense web that passes through apparatuses and institutions, without being exactly localized in them, so too the swarm of points of resistance traverses social stratifications and individual unities.[10]

How can one effectively respond to Foucault's unstringing of Lawrence's rainbow? After all, we, too, are implicated in a discourse that exceeds and subverts our understanding. This, above all else, we understand from reading Foucault.

## II

Perhaps the only thing that one can do in this context is re-pose the Lawrence question by tracing our genealogy back to Lawrence and his most important work, *Women in Love*. In that way the text, I think, can be seen as anticipating and so subsuming Foucault's position on human sexuality. What this implies about the nature of contemporary criticism must be left for future discussion.

Lawrence presents a problem primarily because he appears to be both a modern continuator of the Romantic project of revising traditional religious ideas in terms of secular values and the finest representative of that modern tradition of writers, artists, and thinkers who would destroy the old so as to liberate the radically new. M. H. Abrams in *Natural Supernaturalism* argues the former position as follows:

> Much of what distinguishes writers I call "Romantic" derives from the fact that they undertook, whatever their religious creed or lack of creed, to save traditional concepts, schemes, and values which had been based on the relation of the Creator to his creatures and creation, but to reformulate them within the prevailing two-term system of subject and object, ego and non-ego, the human mind or consciousness and its transactions with nature. Despite their displacement from a supernatural to a natural frame of reference, however, the ancient problems, terminology, and ways of thinking about human nature and history survived, as the implicit distinctions and categories through which even radically secular writers saw themselves and their world, and as the presuppositions and forms of their thinking about the condition, the milieu, the essential values and aspirations, and the history and destiny of the individual and of mankind. . . . What Lawrence has done, in his unique and haunting [works] is to revise the Scriptural account of the fall and apocalypse. . . .[11]

And Philip Rieff argues the latter position on Lawrence in his introduction to *Psychoanalysis and the Unconscious* and *Fantasia of the Unconscious:*

> Lawrence shows himself as the most genuine of modern heresiarchs, chief and father—although only long after his death— over all the little heresiarchs: father-killers, ambivalent mother-lovers, culture-breakers, all those professional youngsters who

swarm the literary horizon looking for an older generation with some left-over self-images that might be good for smashing. Lawrence sensed how thoroughly even his elders had constructed their own morals to meet the new criterion of obsolescence. In his rage at the tyrannous permissiveness and publicity of modern life he is truly the revolutionary of the private life.[12]

Obviously, both Abrams and Rieff are seeing similar things. The terms in which they couch their arguments suggest as much. Where they differ is in their interpretation and evaluation of the essential Lawrence. Is he essentially one of the last Romantics, as Abrams defines the term, or is he the premier revolutionary of the private life, as Rieff claims? Or is he only an uneasy amalgam of both tendencies, like one of his own characters who he asserted were as changeable as the allotropic states of a primal element like carbon?[13] Perhaps Foucault is right and Lawrence is just another example of the modern discourse on human sexuality at work, which combines all the salient features of the religious rite of confession with the new *scientia sexualis* of Freud and Havelock Ellis?

What I want to propose in opposition to these views of Lawrence is that in his finest work, in *Women in Love,* Lawrence is an apocalyptic ironist who says, in effect, a plague on all your houses. In his portrayal of Birkin and his prophetic anality, and in his presentation of Ursula's complex response to him, Lawrence undermines the claims upon his textual projects of both his religious heritage and the increasingly secularized modern world. For Birkin is a latter-day version of Edward Carpenter, the Edwardian prophet of human sexual freedom who is given Lawrence's own features in *Women in Love.* Lawrence shows us that Birkin's authority is radically suspect. Not only is he vulnerable to Ursula's penetrating remarks—"She hated the Salvator Mundi touch"[14]—but he is the familiar compound ghost of displaced religiosity and self-conscious will-to-knowledge (as Foucault would put it) that haunts us all.

Edward Carpenter was an enormously influential late Victorian and Edwardian prophet of human sexual freedom, whose influence on Lawrence and his youthful circle of friends in the Midlands was particularly considerable.[15] Carpenter confounded Christian symbolism, Nietzschean speculations on the *übermensch,* esoteric lore, and the latest developments in the physiology of sex into a heady potion. He prophesied that the future of the earth would belong to an androgynous race of supermen who would reorganize society into freely loving democratic groups. It was as if all men might become in part Walt Whitman, all women Sappho. The two most important of Carpenter's works are *Love's Coming of Age* and *The Art of Creation,* for in them Carpenter repeatedly described the future brand of relations between the sexes in the following terms:

> A marriage so free, so spontaneous, that it would allow of wide excursions of the pair from each other, in common or even in separate objects of work and interest, and yet would hold them all the time in the bond of absolute sympathy, would by its very freedom be all the more poignantly attractive and by its very scope and breadth all the richer and more vital—would be in a sense indestructible, like the relation of two suns which, revolving in fluent and rebounding curves, only recede from each other in order to return again with renewed swiftness into close proximity—and which together blend their rays into the glory of one double star.[16]

Carpenter saw in the increasingly uncertain natures and minds of sensitive and sickly young men signs of the coming times. These men were for Carpenter forerunners or prototypes of the master type that would renew the earth.

Birkin is an extremely close replica of Carpenter's prototype, which itself was created largely in the latter's own image. Birkin possesses an extremely fluid and unstable personality:

> He affected to be quite ordinary, perfectly and marvellously commonplace. And he did it so well, taking the tone of his surroundings, adjusting himself quickly to his interlocutor and his circumstance, that he achieved a verisimilitude of ordinary commonplaceness that usually propitiated his onlookers for the moment, disarmed them from attacking his singleness. . . . he played with situations like a man on a tight-rope: but always on a tight-rope, pretending nothing but ease. [P. 14]

Birkin is capable of such radical changes from moment to moment, from one extreme position to another, from solemn preachiness to mock solemnity and self-disgusting silence, that he is said to be not a man at all by the Italian Contessa who visits Breadleby to attend Hermione's party, but "a chameleon, a creature of change" (p. 85). Birkin is so much a creature of change that he is a connoisseur of decadence and dissolution: sick himself, he appreciates the various forms of sickness in all those around him: "That dark river of dissolution. You see it rolls in us . . . the black river of corruption. And our flowers are of this—our sea-born Aphrodite, all our white phosphorescent flowers of sensuous perfection, all our reality, nowadays" (p. 164). And finally, Birkin even speaks of his salvation, the only kind he can now imagine, in terms of a reimagined marital relation that is clearly drawn from Carpenter's idea of mystic conjunction:

> What I want is a strange conjunction with you" [he tells Ursula]— "not meeting and mingling; you are quite right:—but an equilibrium, a pure balance of two single beings—as the stars balance each other. [P. 139]

> I meant two single equal stars balanced in conjunction—— . . .It is the law of creation. One is committed. One must commit oneself to a conjunction with the other—for ever. But it is not selfless—it is a maintaining of the self in mystic balance and integrity—like a star balanced with another star. [Pp. 142, 144]

Ursula naturally wonders after hearing this, as we do, whether Birkin means for her to be no more than a white dwarf companion of that blue giant who wants an intimate relationship with the god of the mines, Gerald Crich.

I do not want to leave the impression that Birkin is merely the enthusiastic Carpenter updated for more pessimistic times, given a futuristic glitter.[17] Rather, I want to suggest that Birkin represents that compound of religious and scientific ideas, given a Laurentian twist, which threatens to subsume Lawrence's creative life. Lawrence must exorcise this demon by means of this kind of ironic exposure—and he will continue to do so in ever more virulent forms in such later works as *Aaron's Rod, Kangaroo,* and *The Plumed Serpent* until he emerges free of this incubus in the beautiful final works, *The Man Who Died* and the death poems. Lawrence must repeatedly shatter the image of that would-be idol, Birkin/Carpenter, much as Birkin must stone the image of the moon ceaselessly re-forming on the surface of the surging waters in the "Moony" chapter of *Women in Love.*

### III

One of the most effective and most neglected examples of how Lawrence accomplishes this creative feat of self-destruction occurs—at least in part—in the chapter from *Women in Love* called "Sunday Evening." Earlier that day Ursula has returned from the disastrous Water Party on the Crich estate, where Gerald's sister, Diana, and Doctor Brindell have drowned in a senseless boating accident that reveals the fate facing the entire Crich family and the class to which it belongs. Birkin and Ursula have recognized their love for each other, and she longs passionately for his presence at the Brangwen home.

But by the end of the day on Sunday she has drifted into a mood of total resignation, a complete letting go, an acquiescence to the universal flux, and a new appreciation of "the illimitable space of death" as the one last great mystery left unspoiled by modern man and his will to master the earth by translating God's relation to his creation into purely human terms, and in so doing botching and soiling everything with his science, technology, and commercialism:

> But what a joy! What a gladness to think that whatever humanity did, it could not seize hold of the kingdom of death, to nullify that. The sea they turned into a murderous alley and a soiled road of commerce, disputed like the dirty land of a city every inch of it. The air they claimed too, shared it up, parcelled it out to certain owners, they trespassed in the air to fight for it. Everything was gone, walled in, with spikes on top of the walls, and one must ignominiously creep between the spiky walls through a labyrinth of life. [P. 185]

Only death presents Ursula with a "window" onto a prospect of ultimate purification and renewal—of the earth purged of human kind. Even the mind and the body's most secret and sacred mysteries have been invaded, interrogated, and colonized in the name of human knowledge, mastery, and profit.

> Whatever life might be, it could not take away death, the inhuman transcendent death. Oh, let us ask no question of it, what it is or is not. To know is human, and in death we do not know, we are not human. And the joy of this compensates for all the bitterness of knowledge and the sordidness of our humanity. In death we shall not be human, and we shall not know. The promise of this is our heritage, we look forward like heirs to their majority. [P. 186]

The fatal beauty of *Women in Love* occurs when Ursula, rather than Birkin, speaks like this, we are tempted to agree with her that both the Romantic projects of natural supernaturalism and the modern will-to-knowledge have even destroyed the private life: nothing is left but the kingdom of death.

What happens next is that Birkin arrives at the Brangwen home just as Ursula's younger brother and sister, Billy and Dora, are going to bed. Birkin is wonderful to the children, so much so that Billy becomes "angelic like a cherub boy, or like an acolyte" under the ministerings of Birkin (one of Carpenter's signs of the prototype). But Dora becomes "like a tiny Dryad that will not be touched" (p. 187). The children thereby clearly objectify in the scene the moods of Birkin and Ursula. For Ursula now hates Birkin with a passionate intensity that transports and transfigures her. Ursula sees in Birkin the idolization of death that she herself has just given in to. She even transforms him into an image to occupy the center of "the illimitable space of death":

> She saw him, how he was motionless and ageless, like some crouching idol, some image of a deathly religion. He looked round at her, and his face, very pale and unreal, seemed to gleam with a whiteness almost phosphorescent. [P. 188]

Birkin becomes for her now a crystaline beam from the underworld in opposition to her "pure dart of hate, her white flame of essential hate" (p. 190). She has been reborn in his presence as an avenging Persephone that would destroy his would-be phosphorescent Pluto. These are star-crossed lovers with a vengeance.

What has happened here in this chapter of *Women in Love?* A simple answer would be to say that Birkin, because he threatens Ursula's self-indulgent love of death (the only way she can conceive of her freedom), must be seen as deathly. He threatens to kill her death, and replace it with a relation with life. But such an argument would overlook the fact that Ursula is not just projecting onto Birkin her own recent obsession so that she might shed another of her sicknesses. Birkin is consistently associated in the novel with images of death, as indicated earlier. A better answer would be to say that Lawrence has shown Ursula in transition from an idolization of the ultimate vacancy of death to the radical critique of such idolization when it is embodied for her in the person of Birkin. This critique leaves her "quite lost and dazed, really dead to her own life," and yet transformed by her "hate . . . so pure and gem-like" (p. 190)—a demonic parody of Pater's aestheticism, his privileged moment of purely disinterested vision. Where does this leave the reader and Lawrence? Lawrence has established "the illimitable space of death" as the last refuge of the transcendent religious ideal and, at the same time, he has undermined this refuge by exposing Birkin—made in the image of Carpenter's prototype of the androgynous *übermensch*—as the would-be prince of this kingdom—in Ursula's and our eyes. What is this peculiarly self-canceling rhetorical gesture that subverts what it would set up by identifying it with what is thought to be its antithesis?

This textual phenomenon is like de Man's irony. But I would contend that it is not an exclusively linguistic thing, and that it is characteristic of modernist literature in general. It is harnessed by Lawrence, however, rather than being, as Foucault would have it, set loose within the discourse of human sexuality as the will-to-knowledge ceaselessly transforming the constellation of discursive practices of the West in an eternal recurrence of the Same. Lawrence dramatizes in his novel the various forms of revisionary decadence from Gerald Crich's translation of the "mystic word harmony into the practical word organisation" (p. 220) to Loerke's aesthetics of the machine (pp. 421–22), and passes a last judgment upon them all, especially upon that most prevalent form that delights in the expression of an apocalyptic resentment. Lawrence is thus left with nothing at all, with only the imaginary focal point that stands at the center of all these condemnations, like "the illimitable space of death."

Unlike his critical heirs, however, Lawrence refuses finally to name the resultant void, for even death is undone as a name in "Sunday Evening," as we have seen. He does not call it "irony," or "discourse" or "différance," or "angst." And his "dark sun" is a designation that would explode the very idea of exploiting the abysses of paradox, ambiguity, and rhetoric, however conceived. The reader is left, as is Birkin, and presumably Lawrence himself, feeling like a modern version of Milton's Satan:

> To him, the wonder of this transit [to the Continent] was overwhelming. He was falling through a gulf of infinite darkness, like a meteorite plunging across the chasm between the worlds. The world was torn in two, and he was plunging like an unlit star through the ineffable rift. What was beyond was not yet for him. He was overcome by the trajectory. [P. 379]

As Joyce Carol Oates has argued, *Women in Love* is Lawrence's *Götterdämmerung*.[18] Through the wondrous power of the negative, Lawrence smashes "the old idols of ourselves" (p. 47) to make room for the coming of new life—in whatever nonhuman form it might take:

> "Well, if mankind is destroyed, if our race is destroyed like Sodom, and there is this beautiful evening with the luminous land and trees, I am satisfied. That which informs it all is there, and can never be lost. After all, what is mankind but just one expression of the incomprehensible." [P. 52]

But, of course, this very attitude is called into question repeatedly, especially when Loerke and Gudrun delight in imagining the future of the earth as a cosmic catastrophe, blown apart into two equal halves by some ultimate explosive (p. 444).

Another way of putting this repetitive self-cancelation that defines the structure of the novel is to say that Lawrence sets up an opposition here between the fatal action of Western man that has transformed the earth and himself into a standing reserve of material for his designs and the pathetic reaction of those who attempt to critique, or to transcend, or to escape this fate in their various ways. For such reaction always ends up only repeating the crime in a more systematic fashion in yet another area of human existence. What Lawrence leaves the reader, then, is not de Man's linguistic machine, or Foucault's discursive network, but simply "nothing" at all:

> "Of course," he [Birkin] said, "Julius [the Bertrand Russell figure] is somewhat insane. On one hand he's had religious mania, and on the other, he is fascinated by obscenity. Either he is a pure servant, washing the feet of Christ, or else he is making obscene drawings of Jesus—action and reaction—and between the two, nothing. He is really insane. . . . It's the old story—action and reaction, and nothing between." [P. 88]

Mrs. Lawrence's son never put the nature of his love any better: "just one expression of the incomprehensible."

## Notes

1. Paul de Man, *Allegories of Reading: Figural Language in Rousseau, Nietzsche, Rilke, and Proust* (New Haven, Conn.: Yale University Press, 1979), pp. 173–74.

2. Ibid., p. 187.

3. Paul de Man, "Shelley Disfigured," *Deconstruction and Criticism* (New York: Seabury Press, 1979), p. 69.

4. See Harold Bloom, *The Flight to Lucifer: A Gnostic Fantasy* (New York: Farrar, Straus & Giroux, 1979); Edward W. Said, *Orientalism* (New York: Pantheon, 1978); and Jacques Derrida, *Spurs: Nietzsche's Styles*, trans. Barbara Harlow (Chicago: University of Chicago Press, 1979). See as well two of my review articles: "The Romance of Interpretation: A 'Postmodern' Critical Style," *boundary 2* 8, no. 2 (1980): 259–83, and "The Freedom of the Master?", *Contemporary Literature* 2, no. 4 (1980): 649–61.

5. De Man, *Allegories of Reading,* p. 288.

6. Cited in ibid., p. 298.

7. Ibid., p. 301.

8. Michel Foucault, *The History of Sexuality: An Introduction,* trans. Robert Hurley (New York: Pantheon, 1978), p. 45.

9. Ibid., p. 157.

10. Ibid., p. 96.

11. M. H. Abrams, *Natural Supernaturalism* (New York: Norton, 1971), pp. 13 and 324.

12. Philip Rieff, introduction to D. H. Lawrence's *Psychoanalysis and the Unconscious* and *Fantasia of the Unconscious* (New York: Viking, 1960), p. xiii.

13. See "Extracts from Letters," *D. H. Lawrence: Selected Literary Criticism,* ed. Anthony Beal (New York: Viking, 1966), pp. 17–18. The reference is to the famous letter of 5 June 1914 to Edward Garnett. For commentary on this letter, see Frank Kermode, *D. H. Lawrence* (New York: Viking, 1973), pp. 27–29.

14. D. H. Lawrence, *Women in Love* (New York: Viking, 1960), p. 121. Hereafter all references to the novel will be given in the text.

15. See Emile Delavenay, *D. H. Lawrence and Edward Carpenter: A Study in Edwardian Transition* (New York: Taplinger, 1971). I am greatly indebted to this excellent study. However, Delavenay is concerned with the relation of Lawrence's ideas to Carpenter's. He draws no formal or literary conclusion from the relationship.

16. Ibid., p. 91.

17. See Lawrence's letter to Edward Garnett of 5 June 1914.

18. Joyce Carol Oates, "Lawrence's *Götterdämmerung:* The Tragic Vision of *Women in Love,*" *Critical Inquiry* 4 (Spring 1978): 559–88.

# Pragmatics in Wonderland

## Michael Hancher

### University of Minnesota

ALICE was beginning to get very tired of sitting by her sister on the bank, and of having nothing to do: once or twice she had peeped into the book her sister was reading, but it had no pictures or conversations in it, 'and what is the use of a book,' thought Alice, 'without pictures or conversations?'"[1] Alice would have liked *Alice in Wonderland,* which opens with this sentence, because it contains many pictures and conversations. She would have liked *Through the Looking-Glass* for the same reason. More than a few of the pictures show conversations. A typical example is figure 1 (page 166), which illustrates the following exchange:

> "Your hair wants cutting," said the Hatter. He had been looking at Alice for some time with great curiosity, and this was his first speech.
> "You should learn not to make personal remarks," Alice said with some severity: "it's very rude."[2]

The same picture could illustrate this conversation almost as well:

> "Have you guessed the riddle yet?" the Hatter said, turning to Alice again.
> "No, I give it up," Alice replied. "What's the answer?"
> "I haven't the slightest idea," said the Hatter.
> "Nor I," said the March Hare.
> Alice sighed wearily. "I think you might do something better with the time," she said, "than wasting it in asking riddles that have no answers." [AW 7]

Figure 2 (page 166) shows a different set of conversationalists just a few moments before this odd exchange takes place:

**Figure 1. Sir John Tenniel's illustration of Alice at the tea party, from** *Alice's Adventures in Wonderland.*

**Figure 2. Alice and the two Queens in conversation, one of Tenniel's illustrations for** *Through the Looking-Glass.*

The Red Queen broke the silence by saying, to the White Queen, "I invite you to Alice's dinner-party this afternoon."

The White Queen smiled feebly, and said "And I invite *you*."

"I didn't know I was to have a party at all," said Alice; "but, if there *is* to be one, I think *I* ought to invite the guests." [*LG* 9]

Much of the verbal humor of the *Alice* books is like this, and only some of it can be explained in terms of such traditional formalist or autonomous linguistic concepts as semantic and syntactic ambiguity, fallacies of logic or of reference, and the like. The two-dimensional linguistic hierarchy cited by one student of Carroll's wordplay—"phone, phoneme, morph, morpheme, phrase, sentence, block of unified discourse"—is useless to explain what is so funny about the interaction among these queens; and no narrowly logical analysis can justly gauge the madness or sanity of the Mad Hatter's remarks.[3]

The relevant factors will have to be looked for on a different plane. These factors involve not the structure of logic or the structure of language so much as the *use* of language—what has come to be known as "pragmatics." Recent pragmatic theory has been especially sensitive to the "rules and regulations" that govern conversation.[4] We might hope that it will help us understand the curious world that Alice discovers down the rabbit hole and behind the glass.

To put the matter in its most general terms: humor is often a matter of "breaking the rules"—whatever the rules might be. *Some* humor turns on the breaking of pragmatic language rules, or on their faulty execution.[5] In Wonderland both constitutive and regulative language rules get fractured in a variety of funny ways. This essay will consider a few representative examples.

Of course, there is as yet no complete theory of pragmatics, but there are several partial and overlapping suggestions that seem promising. One of the oldest of these is J. L. Austin's speech-act theory, refined by his student John Searle.[6] Much of the comedy of the *Alice* books is illocutionary comedy, explicable in Austin's and Searle's terms. A good example is the already cited exchange between Alice and the two other queens. When the Red Queen and the White Queen invite each other to Alice's dinner party, their speech acts are essentially "misinvocations" (as Austin would say) of the inviting procedure. If Alice were in the real world it would be perfectly in order for her to object, as she does here, "I didn't know I was to have a party at all; but, if there *is* to be one, I think *I* ought to invite the guests." In making this objection, Alice recognizes the double infelicity that causes the Queens' invitations to misfire ("inappropriate circumstances," and "inappropriate persons").[7] What she never does quite grasp is that her rules, and our rules, and Austin's rules, by which we count such infelicities, don't really apply in the brave new world that she finds herself in.

After the caucus race, when the Dodo hands out the prizes, he awards Alice a thimble that happens to be hers already; in fact, he has just gotten her to hand it over. Alice correctly finds "the whole thing very absurd" (*AW* 3); and the absurdity that she detects is illocutionary. Austin himself cites a parallel example of misinvocation: the utterance " 'I give,' said when it is not mine to give."[8] When Carroll rewrote *Alice in Wonderland* in a special nursery version, one meant for children under five years old, he knew that the pragmatic competence of even very young children would enable them to spot such an absurdity— at least with the benefit of a little philosophical coaching. "Wasn't *that* a curious sort of present to give her?" he comments to the toddlers.

> Suppose they wanted to give *you* a birthday-present, would you rather they should go to your toy-cupboard, and pick out your nicest doll, and say "Here, my love, here's a lovely birthday-present for you!" or would you like them to give you something *new*, something that *didn't* belong to you before?[9]

Austin's analysis of defective giving is more succinct than this, but the point is the same.

Creatures who have such trouble with more or less explicit performative procedures are not likely to fare better with inexplicit or indirect speech acts, and, in fact, a minor leitmotif of the *Alice* books is failure to secure uptake caused by surface illocutionary ambiguity.

When Humpty Dumpty makes an obscure reference to his "un-birthday present" Alice asks for an explanation by saying, "with a puzzled air," the words "I beg your pardon?", but Humpty mistakes her *request* for an *apology* and responds with the unapt reassurance "I'm not offended" (*LG* 6). When the White King gives an obscure explanation of why he needs two messengers, Alice asks "I beg your pardon?", but the King can't see beyond the explicit surface verb: " 'It isn't respectable to beg,' said the King. 'I only meant that I didn't understand,' said Alice" (*LG* 7).

In both these examples the hearer grasps the locutionary act but mistakes the illocutionary act. Sometimes the illocutionary act may be unclear because the locutionary act is unclear. When the Sheep calls out "Feather!" to Alice as Alice rows the boat, she completely misses the directive (imperative) illocutionary force of the utterance because she doesn't know that *feather* is a verb with special application to the use of oars. "This didn't sound like a remark that needed any answer," Carroll tells us, "so Alice said nothing, but pulled away" (*LG* 5). Of course, "Feather!" was not a remark at all, but a directive, and a directive that required not an answer but a physical response.

The Sheep's directive to feather misfires because it is not *heard as* a directive; that is, it does not "secure uptake." Still other directives misfire in the *Alice* books because of presupposition-failures that Austin calls "infelicities."

When the Queen of Hearts orders the executioner to behead the Cheshire Cat, which at that point is only a grinning head, the man reasonably enough objects "that you couldn't cut off a head unless there was a body to cut it off from." That is a sound speech-act objection, which he immediately obscures with fresh absurdities: "he had never had to do such a thing before, and he wasn't going to begin at *his* time of life" (*AW* 8). His own illocutionary activity shifts here from *objecting* to *refusing*, and the new refusal is as nonsensical as the original order, for one of the preconditions on refusing to perform an action is that the action be voluntary. If an action is impossible it can hardly be voluntary, and this particular action is impossible by his own account.

The Queen, of course, gave her nonsensical order in good faith, if somewhat negligently, for she had not seen the Cat and did not know how strange it was. In this respect she differs from the March Hare, who issues a similarly defective directive to Alice in what appears to be bad faith:

> "Have some wine," the March Hare said in an encouraging tone.
> Alice looked all round the table, but there was nothing on it but tea. "I don't see any wine," she remarked.
> "There isn't any," said the March Hare.
> "Then it wasn't very civil of you to offer it," said Alice angrily.
> "It wasn't very civil of you to sit down without being invited," said the March Hare. [*AW* 7]

The topic of civility is one we must return to later. What matters here is that the March Hare's directive to Alice fails in one of its felicity conditions; that is, the condition that she be thought to be able to do what she is thereby told to do.[10]

Almost immediately the Mad Hatter pulls another, and similar, presuppositional rug out from under Alice by putting to her the famous bogus riddle, "Why is a raven like a writing-desk?" After some byplay Alice learns enough about what is going on to put the very reasonable objection, "I think you might do something better with the time than wasting it in asking riddles that have no answers." In putting such a riddle to Alice—that is, in directing her to say the unsayable—the Mad Hatter perpetrates an infelicitous illocutionary act, whether wittingly or unwittingly.

Much hangs on the difference. If the Mad Hatter is not in his right mind, his nonsensical speech act is as naive as the Queen's nonsensical command. But suppose for the moment that the Mad Hatter is not wholly mad, even as the March Hare may not be merely lunatic when he tells Alice to have some wine that isn't there. In such a case the speech-act model of Austin and Searle temporarily fails us, and we need to refer to some other, more inclusive, pragmatic theory.

A useful model in such a case is H. P. Grice's model of conversational implicature. Grice builds his model on the proposition that participants in conversation understand the following imperative to be in force: "Make your conversational contribution such as is required, at the stage at which it occurs, by the accepted purpose or direction of the talk exchange in which you are engaged." This he calls the "Cooperative Principle." Specific subrules or maxims spell out in more detail what the Cooperative Principle requires of a speaker. Grice's general point is that any infringement of the Cooperative Principle will be noticeable as such, and will therefore be available to the speaker as a means of signaling information implicitly, rather than explicitly (rather, that is, than by virtue of the meaning assignable to the utterance by syntactic and semantic conventions alone).[11]

Grice constructed his Cooperative Principle and conversational maxims with representative (that is, assertive) speech acts mainly in mind, but similar regulative rules would cover directives like the two we are considering.[12] In particular, the super-maxim of Quality, "Try to make your contribution [to the conversation] one that is true," can be readily expanded to cover performative utterances, in some such fashion as this: "Try to make your contribution one that is true, *or that has its presuppositions fulfilled.*" I suspect that in directing Alice to have wine that isn't there, and in asking her a riddle that has no answer, the March Hare and the Mad Hatter both are *deliberately* breaching such a maxim.

If that is the case, any one of several Gricean behaviors may be going on.

At first, both the Hare and the Hatter "quietly and unostentatiously VIOLATE [the] maxim," with the intention to mislead.

No doubt they also intend their presuppositional defects to be quickly discovered, and to that extent they may be said to "FLOUT" the maxim, that is, "BLATANTLY fail to fulfill it."

By flouting a maxim one can "EXPLOIT" it: that is, one can thereby suggest an unstated message ("implicatum") that the hearer may be expected rationally to recover from "between the lines" of the utterance as a way of neutralizing the apparent threat to the presumption that the speaker has been observing the Cooperative Principle—such threat arising from the unmistakable breach of the maxim. Such maxim-exploiting suggestion Grice calls "conversational implicature."

If the Hare and the Hatter are indeed flouting the maxim of Quality on directives so as to implicate something, in both cases the implicatum might plausibly be that they dislike Alice's behavior and want her to go back where she came from.

That second account is hard to distinguish from a third, which is that in perpetrating their bogus directives on Alice they "OPT OUT" from the operation of both the maxim of Quality *and also* the general Cooperative Principle, in effect temporarily banishing Alice from their community. Profound hostility toward the hearer can be even better expressed by opting out of the rule of the Cooperative Principle than by implicating hostility through maxim-exploitation within the rule of that principle, though in the end the "message" comes to much the same thing. (This particular embarrassment of descriptions is special to utterances that are calculated so to alienate the hearer from the speaker as to jeopardize the very existence of the conversation.)

All the Gricean maxims come into play—or into nonplay—in Wonderland. The first maxim of Quantity ("Make your contribution as informative as is required") describes what is wrong with the March Hare's watch, which "tells the day of the month, and doesn't tell what o'clock it is!" (*AW* 7). The many obscurantists that Alice encounters—ranging from the Dodo through the White Queen to Humpty Dumpty himself—give the supermaxim of Manner ("Be perspicuous") a thorough going over, not always in the service of some implicature. And the maxim of Relation ("Be relevant") is almost always in jeopardy.

Though much more can be said about Austin in Wonderland and Grice through the Looking-Glass, there are other practical aspects of conversation that require attention. If speech-act theory may be said to articulate the *common law* of conversation, and if implicature theory describes its peculiar *logic*, there are also conversational *economics* and *politics* to reckon with.

By *economics* I mean the science of the circulation of speech within a conversational community, and by *politics* the science that describes the various rights and responsibilities that different members of the conversational community will maintain with respect to one another.

Of course ordinary economics and ordinary politics overlap to a considerable extent: one may be inexplicable without the other. The same is true of conversational economy and conversational policy. Though these twin sociolinguistic sciences are of recent foundation, they should be able to enhance our understanding of some of the language problems that preoccupy Alice on her two strange outings.

Until his death in 1975, Harvey Sacks was the dean of what I have been calling conversational economics. His research into the structure of conversational interaction, and the research of his students and colleagues, provides a formal and analytic account of certain large- and small-scale behaviors that organize ordinary conversation, particularly those affecting at any given moment the distribution of the privilege of speech among the members of the conversational community.[13]

By and large the dialogue represented in literature is a very much simplified version of ordinary spoken dialogue; therefore many of the microanalytic insights of Sacks and his colleagues have no direct application to most literary texts. But some general principles inform all their analyses, both large- and small-scale, and these do have a bearing on the literary representation of the production and experience of conversation.

There are several kinds of economic constraint that determine, to a significant extent, the course and the coherence of any natural dialogue. The most general and systematic of these condition basic intelligibility. For example: No more than one speaker at a time. At least one person speaks at a time. The right and obligation to speak at any given moment may be assigned in an orderly way to a new speaker by the previous speaker (or, in special cases, by *a* previous speaker); failing that, it may be claimed by any speaker at the end of an appropriate stretch of the previous speaker's discourse (technically known as a "transition-relevance place"). In all cases the hearer will certify his attention and understanding by continually providing back-channel or kinesic clues.

All these constraints are exceptionable. From time to time more than one person will speak at once, or no one will speak; from time to time a selected speaker will remain silent, or a person other than the selected speaker will usurp the floor.

But such apparent exceptions confirm the existence of the underlying rules. The silence of a selected speaker who will not speak takes on an interactional and communicative significance that it would lack if the speaker had not been selected. The relative brevity of most simultaneous discourse in conversation testifies to the prohibition that has been violated. And so on.

Aside from such general constraints there are particular constraints that organize local conversational subroutines, such as greeting, parting, directing-responding, giving-thanking, and so on. Such subroutines typically subsume obligatory pairs of speech acts, called "adjacency pairs," which conversationalists will generate as the occasion requires.

By and large, conversationalists act under the discipline of such constraints without paying them much attention. But, unlike many rules of grammar, such systematic and occasional requirements can readily rise to consciousness, and will do so whenever there is an obvious conversational emergency. So it is that Alice spends a fair amount of time coming to terms with the problem of whose turn it is right then to talk, and responding to unorthodox conversational demands.

Alice's economic distress is made worse by the fact that she is a child. In Wonderland, even as in Victorian England, the role of children in the conversational economy is subject to the whim of adults. The crisis at the end of *Wonderland* comes about when Alice refuses to hold her tongue, as the Queen of Hearts has commanded her to do. In defiantly usurping the floor Alice discovers to her surprise that the Queen and her court are "nothing but a pack of cards" (*AW* 12). The logo-economic advantage of the adult Queen disappears when Alice asserts her own right to speak not as a child but as an adult.

But in *Through the Looking-Glass* the Red Queen makes fresh claims on that lost authority, and sets out to control Alice's access to conversation. After Alice tries to initiate a conversation with her, she rebukes Alice with the maxim "Speak when you're spoken to." Alice has the wit to interpret this rule generally, ignoring its implicit restriction to children and other inferiors. Taking it categorically, she tests its worth as a categorical imperative:

> "But if everybody obeyed that rule," said Alice, who was always ready for a little argument, "and if you only spoke when you were spoken to, and the other person always waited for *you* to begin, you see nobody would ever say anything, so that—"
> "Ridiculous!" cried the Queen. "Why, don't you see, child—" here she broke off with a frown, and, after thinking for a minute, suddenly changed the subject of the conversation. [*LG* 9]

In this exchange Alice focuses on the difficulties that such a categorical rule against speaker self-selection would pose for conversational beginnings. She might go on to note that such a rule would drastically restructure conversational middles, contradicting as it does the Sacks-Schegloff-Jefferson rule 1.b ("For any turn . . . at initial turn-constructional unit's initial transition-relevance place . . . if the turn-so-far is so constructed as not to involve the use of a 'current speaker selects next' technique, self-selection for next speakership may, but need not, be instituted, with first starter acquiring rights to a turn, transfer occurring at that place").[14]

Curiously, the Red Queen repeatedly enjoins Alice to *speak*. This usually happens at one or another juncture that she—that is, the Red Queen—"formulates" as being a slot reserved for the second item of an adjacency pair. More often than not there is something idiosyncratic about her formulation. On first encountering Alice, the Red Queen asks what brought her to the vicinity, and then delays any possible response by retaining the floor to tell her to curtsy while she thinks of what to say. Then, looking at her watch, she instructs Alice, "It's time for you to answer now" (*LG* 2). The sense in which it *is* "time" for the response item of the question-response adjacency pair has of course nothing to do with the absolute chronology of watches and clocks.

At the end of the same chapter the Red Queen imposes her own peculiar sequencing rule on the adjacency pair made up of giving and thanking.

> At the two-yard peg she faced round, and said, "A pawn goes two squares in its first move, you know. So you'll go *very* quickly

> through the Third Square—by railway, I should think—and you'll
> find yourself in the Fourth Square in no time. Well, *that* square
> belongs to Tweedledum and Tweedledee—the Fifth is mostly wa-
> ter—the Sixth belongs to Humpty Dumpty—But you make no re-
> mark?"
> "I—I didn't know I had to make one—just then," Alice faltered
> out.
> "You *should* have said," the Queen went on in a tone of grave
> reproof, "'It's extremely kind of you to tell me all this'—however,
> we'll suppose it said—the Seventh Square is all forest—however,
> one of the Knights will show you the way." [*LG* 2]

Evidently Alice and the Red Queen have different perceptions
of where in the Queen's speech the first "transition-relevance
place" occurs. It must seem to Alice that the Queen had un-
reasonably expected Alice to interrupt her in the middle of a
speaking turn.

Other problems in conversational economy that Alice faces
on her journeys include a considerable number of abnormal
conversational openings (with Humpty Dumpty and with the
Tweedle- brothers, for example), occasional awkward lapses in
the conversation, and an epidemic of poetry recitations that for
the time being effectively block normal access to the floor.

Of course the monopolistic power of poetry is something that
it shares with oratory; so it is fitting to end this brief review of
the economic aspects of conversation in the *Alice* books by notic-
ing that Alice's climactic if incomplete speech act at the end of
*Through the Looking-Glass* is a formal speech, a piece of oratory.
Specifically, it is a speech of thanks, one that is required as the
adjacency-pair complement to the toast to Alice's health that
the Red Queen has just proposed. (In this case the Red Queen's
provoking rebuke is quite orthodox: "'You ought to return
thanks in a neat speech,' the Red Queen said, frowning at Alice
as she spoke.") The responsibility of having the floor all to
herself, of course, proves to be too much for Alice; she loses her
grasp on fantasy altogether, and her dream comes to an abrupt
end (*LG* 9).

But not this essay, for there is still to consider the most inclusive pragmatic science of all, which I have been calling conversational politics, and which is more usually called the theory of
linguistic politeness. An awareness that certain social inhibi-
tions can complicate otherwise straightforward linguistic
routines—syntactic, semantic, and pragmatic alike—has been
gaining ground in the linguistic field for almost a decade. The

relatively informal work of Robin Lakoff in particular greatly
encouraged this development, which recently culminated in the
publication of an elaborate treatise by Penelope Brown and
Stephen Levinson.[15] Like Lakoff, Brown and Levinson argue
that politeness phenomena motivate many details of speech-act
behavior, of conversational implicature, and of conversational
economy.

Again like Lakoff, Brown and Levinson are considerably indebted to Erving Goffman's sociological analyses of interactional behavior. They frame their basic concepts in terms of
what Goffman calls "face," which he defines as "the positive
social value a person effectively claims for himself" in interaction with others.[16] Brown and Levinson distinguish "negative
face," or the desire of a person for freedom from interference,
from "positive face," or the desire of a person "that his wants
[whether fulfilled or not] be desirable to at least some others."
*Negative face* wishes to be let alone; *positive face* wishes to be
flattered or "stroked." Obviously the need for independence
and the need for social sympathy are fundamentally at odds
with each other, which is what makes adolescence something of
a permanent human condition.

Most, if not all, social behaviors threaten one or the other
aspect of either the agent's face or the patient's face. This
generalization, of course, includes the various speech-act behaviors. Directives of all sorts threaten the hearer's negative
face, as do expressions of anger; expressions of disapproval or
dislike threaten the hearer's positive face, as does contradicting
the hearer or interrupting his turn at talk (the latter threatens
negative face also). Such behaviors as expressing thanks or accepting offers threaten the speaker's negative face; confessions
and apologies threaten the speaker's positive face. All such actions—and there are many—Brown and Levinson call *face-
threatening acts,* or *FTAs* for short.

Faced with a desire to perform an FTA, a speaker has five
basic options: (1) don't do it; (2) do it in a deniable way, "off
record," through Gricean conversational implicature (that is,
unconventional circumlocution); (3) do it without mitigation;
(4) do it with mitigation, or "redress," addressed to the hearer's
positive face; (5) do it with mitigation or redress addressed to
the hearer's negative face. In any given context the speaker will
have good reasons to follow one option or another; Brown and
Levinson describe how such reasons are calculated. The fact
that many of the strategic parameters will be known to both

parties sets the stage for considerable revision and second-guessing. There is also always the chance of making a mistake, which can be funny.

All five of the basic strategies are important to the *Alice* books. Because the narrator speaks mainly from Alice's point of view, we learn a good deal about what she thinks as well as about what she says. One of her more recurrent thoughts is that it is better to say nothing at all than to utter an FTA. "Alice thought it would not be civil to say 'No,' though it [a proffered biscuit] wasn't at all what she wanted" (*LG* 2); "Alice didn't want to begin another argument, so she said nothing" (*LG* 6). Reports like these are common. They show that Alice is making some effort to be well behaved.

Though it may be unfair to the other characters (mostly adults) that we are denied sympathetic access to their inner thoughts and feelings, the fact is that they do not seem to be very sparing of FTAs, mitigated or not. "Off with her head!" is only the most obvious example of a "bald-on-record" FTA. Another is the example with which we started: "'Your hair wants cutting,' said the Hatter" to which Alice responds meta- and sociolinguistically, "You should learn not to make personal remarks: it's very rude." (An FTA for an FTA.)

The rule Alice cites is very general, for the notion "personal remarks" includes compliments as well as criticisms. Compliments threaten negative face only. Criticisms threaten positive face, though sometimes (as here) they also carry suggestions of interference, and so threaten both kinds.

A nice instance of an off-record FTA is the reprimand that the Mouse gives the Lory, right after the Mouse has launched into his recitation of "the driest thing I know" (the creatures and Alice are all sopping wet and he wants to dry them off), which is a very dry passage from a political history book for children. The Lory has interjected a criticism of this recitation:

> "Ugh!" said the Lory, with a shiver.
> "I beg your pardon!" said the Mouse, frowning, but *very politely*. "Did you speak?"
> "Not I!" said the Lory, hastily.
> "I thought you did," said the Mouse. "I proceed. 'Edwin and Morcar, the earls of Mercia and Northumbria, declared for him. . . .'" [*AW* 3; emphasis added]

A full analysis of this ordinary schoolroom exchange requires reference to all the pragmatic models we have been considering. First, the Mouse's polite question, "Did you speak?", is openly insincere. In putting it the Mouse can hardly be requesting information, for the facts of the matter are already obvious to him. In Searle's terms, his speech act openly violates the first preparatory condition on questions, "$S$ does not know 'the answer,'" and also, therefore, the sincerity condition on questions, "$S$ wants this information." By flouting the sincerity condition on questioning in this way the Mouse indicates that his supposed "question" is really ironic—that he means something other than what he says.[17] The Lory can tell that this ironic question, in these particular circumstances, actually implicates a reprimand—in particular, a reprimand for having usurped the floor.

In responding as he does with a denial that is superficially a false assertion the Lory does not actually lie, because his violation of Grice's first maxim of Quality, "Do not say what you believe to be false" is overt. (The speaker knows that the hearer knows that the denial is false, and the speaker intends the hearer to recognize that he is not supposed to believe the denial.) In flouting the maxim this way the Lory exploits the Quality maxim to implicate something other than what he says. No doubt this resort to implicature is an off-record politeness strategy designed to shield partially his own negative face from the threat posed by the point of his utterance—which is, I take it, to commit himself to reform his behavior. (As indeed he does thereafter.)

Note that the polite off-record channeling of *both* animals' speech acts, that is, both the Mouse's reprimand and the Lory's response, is calculated to assuage the negative-face wants of the *same* animal (the Lory). This asymmetry has an obvious relation to the asymmetrical power relations that obtain between the two. *Noblesse oblige.*

I should add that the remarkable artificiality of this everyday exchange is a source of its mild humor. The deformation of straightforward procedures that culture requires in the name of politeness is always vulnerable to satire.

For an illustration of how the various redressive actions included under strategies (4) and (5) can mitigate FTAs, consider the following stretch of dialogue, chosen more or less at random. Alice has just finished reciting—or misreciting—"You Are Old, Father William," to the Caterpillar.

"That is not said right," said the Caterpillar.

"Not *quite* right, I'm afraid," said Alice, timidly: "some of the words have got altered."

"It is wrong from beginning to end," said the Caterpillar, decidedly; and there was silence for some minutes.

The Caterpillar was the first to speak.

"What size do you want to be?" it asked.

"Oh, I'm not particular as to size," Alice hastily replied; "only one doesn't like changing so often, you know."

"I *don't* know," said the Caterpillar.

Alice said nothing: she had never been so much contradicted in all her life before, and she felt that she was losing her temper.

"Are you content now?" said the Caterpillar.

"Well, I should like to be a *little* larger, Sir, if you wouldn't mind," said Alice: "three inches is such a wretched height to be."

"It is a very good height indeed!" said the Caterpillar angrily, rearing itself upright as it spoke (it was exactly three inches high).

"But I'm not used to it!" pleaded poor Alice in a piteous tone. And she thought to herself "I wish the creatures wouldn't be so easily offended!" [*AW* 5]

The Caterpillar's criticism, "That is not said right," is a bald-on-record FTA.

Alice's response, "Not *quite* right, I'm afraid: some of the words have got altered," includes two quantity hedges ("quite" and "some") and a deleted-agent passive-voice impersonalization strategy ("have got altered"), all of which mitigate the threat her concession poses to *her* positive face. These self-protective gestures are details of a larger positive-politeness strategy, calculated to anoint the *Caterpillar*'s positive face, which Brown and Levinson identify as "token agreement."

The Caterpillar's renewal of the FTA ("It is wrong from beginning to end") leaves Alice speechless, until it changes the subject, and asks her, "What size do you want to be?" Though this question, like all questions, involves a mild threat to the addressee's negative face, it more obviously expresses a degree of sympathy with her positive-face wants.

"Oh, I'm not particular as to size," Alice replies, in a remark calculated to be relatively unthreatening. But she continues: "only one doesn't like changing so often, you know." Such use of the impersonal "one" is a stock negative-politeness strategy, and saying "you know" in this way invokes what Brown and Levinson call a "common ground" between the speaker and the hearer—a reliable positive-politeness strategy. This double redressive action works to mitigate the threat to the Caterpillar's negative face that is presented by the complaint which Alice is making. (All complaints tend to impinge on the existential freedom of the addressee, even if he is not responsible for having brought about the offending condition.)

But the Caterpillar rejects Alice's polite claim of solidarity by flatly contradicting, "I *don't* know." This action doubly threatens Alice's positive face (both as a contradiction and as a denial of solidarity); so she quite characteristically lapses into silence in order to avoid losing her temper—which according to Brown and Levinson would be an FTA to her own positive face, as well as an obvious FTA to the Caterpillar.

When the Caterpillar finally puts a query, "Are you content now?", which in context anoints Alice's positive face almost as much as his previous question did, Alice feels emboldened to articulate her wants in the form of an indirect request: "Well, I should like to be a *little* larger, Sir, if you wouldn't mind." In the first clause of this utterance Alice (elliptically) asserts the fulfillment of the sincerity condition on requests ("*S* wants *H* to do *A*"), which is a politely indirect way of putting a request.[18] The potential threat posed to the Caterpillar's negative face by such a request is further mitigated by the fact that even Alice's assertion of the condition is elliptical; that is, Alice withholds any mention of the Caterpillar until the next clause.

The quantity hedge ("a *little* larger") works to minimize the imposition, further protecting the Caterpillar's negative face, and the honorific "Sir" flatters its positive face. The final hedge, "if you wouldn't mind," makes a further concession to the Caterpillar's negative-face wants.

Unfortunately Alice is so very cautious as to add to all these maneuvers yet another negative-politeness strategy, number six in Brown and Levinson's schema: "Apologize." The particular kind of apology that Alice undertakes falls under the rubric, "Give overwhelming reasons." As Brown and Levinson describe this strategy, the imposing speaker "can claim that he has compelling reasons for doing the FTA (for example, his own incapacity), thereby implying that normally he wouldn't dream of infringing H's negative face." And so Alice ventures this last remark as an apology and justification: "three inches is such a wretched height to be."

> "It is a very good height indeed!" said the Caterpillar angrily, rearing itself upright as it spoke (it was exactly three inches high).
> "But I'm not used to it!" pleaded poor Alice in a piteous tone. And she thought to herself "I wish the creatures wouldn't be so easily offended."

What Alice offered in good faith as a concession to the Cater-pillar's negative face, it took as a threat to its positive face. She fails to grasp why; children are always slow to appreciate the hypersensitiveness of others concerning their positive-face needs. There are similar scenes of inadvertent cruelty else-where in the book, though they usually involve negative FTAs, which can be even crueller than positive ones. For example, Alice's efforts to engage the Mouse in friendly conversation repeatedly founder on the mention of one or another of her rat-catching pets. Alice ignores the old polite-conversation maxim known to Sancho Panza and Lord Chesterfield alike: "Don't mention a rope in the house of a hanged man."

If Alice's incivility to the Caterpillar were willful, it might be funny, in a slapstick sort of way. But being negligent, and not willful, it is funny in a different way, having more to do with irony (in the general sense of the word), and peripety. (By *peripety* I mean not just a change of fortune, but an action that turns upon itself, effecting a result which is the reverse of what was intended.[19])

On her journeys underground and on the other side of the looking-glass, Childe Alice undergoes many ordeals, most of which are verbal and social. I think that the various examples I have cited show that pragmatic theory can describe these or-deals with considerable precision. In particular, the recently developed theory of linguistic politeness—which itself incorpo-rates major elements of speech-act theory, of the theory of conversational implicature, and of interactional analysis—fits the text remarkably well. The question is whether this is just a happy coincidence, a random isomorphism of text and method, or whether politeness theory may be pertinent to other texts of our culture.

There is some evidence that it may be just a coincidence. Often, maybe even more often than the examples that I have quoted suggest, the narrator and characters of the *Alice* books will make explicit mention of prescriptive norms of linguistic politeness and civility. Perhaps *Alice is* a sport, a linguistic-politeness book, rather as *Coriolanus* is said to be a speech-act play. But I doubt that this is the case. *Alice* may be somewhat unusual in the extent to which it foregrounds the problems of polite verbal behavior, but it is not unusual in the extent to which it shows characters defining, negotitating, and renegotiating their social identities in subtly adjusted verbal interaction.

In his essay containing a virtuoso speech-act reading of *Coriolanus*, Stanley Fish has suggested that speech-act theory is useful only for interpreting works that are mainly and already "about" the importance of performative speech-act behavior (promising, banishing, renouncing, and the like).[20] This may be too narrow a formulation, but it does make a point. The speech-act net produced by the standard theory has for some time now been loosely woven, suitable only for trapping the biggest performative game. Politeness theory, such as Brown and Levinson provide, is much more tightly woven, and is much more able to capture subtle movements in the shared discourse that constitutes any society and its members. The fact that such matters are fully political and ideological does not lessen the interest of the theory.

One last observation. When I was in college, my professors told me and my fellow students that something called "tone" was very important to the reading of poetry. They were never very clear about what "tone" was, exactly, no clearer than were their own New Critical mentors. I did learn that it was supposed to define in some way the author's attitude to his reader, or the speaker's attitude to his audience. Of course they were right to say that these are important subjects, and I think that at last we are in a position to begin to say how and why this is so.

## Notes

1. Lewis Carroll, *Alice's Adventures in Wonderland and Through the Looking-Glass and What Alice Found There*, ed. R. L. Green, Oxford English Novels (London: Oxford University Press, 1971), p. 9. Later quotations will be drawn from this edition, cited by volume *(AW, LG)* and chapter only.

Preliminary work on this article was made possible by a grant from the National Endowment for the Humanities.

2. AW 7. Carroll later specified of this picture, "He [the Hatter] has just got up to say to Alice 'Your hair wants cutting!'" *The Nursery "Alice": Containing Twenty Coloured Enlargements from Tenniel's Illustrations to "Alice's Adventures in Wonderland" with Text Adapted to Nursery Readers by Lewis Carroll* (1890; reprint ed., New York: McGraw-Hill, 1966), p. 40.

3. Robert D. Sutherland, *Language and Lewis Carroll*, Janua Linguarum, Series Major, 26 (The Hague: Mouton, 1970), p. 85. The following works also explore linguistic and logical anomalies in the *Alice* books, but are not equipped to discuss most of the aspects to be discussed here: Peter Alexander, "Logic and the Humour of Lewis Carroll," *Proceedings of the Leeds Philosophical and Literary Society* 6 (1944–47): 551–66. Elizabeth

Sewell, *The Field of Nonsense* (London: Chatto, 1952). Roger W. Holmes, "The Philosopher's *Alice in Wonderland*," *Antioch Review* 19 (1959): 133–49. *The Annotated Alice,* ed. Martin Gardner (New York: Clarkson N. Potter, 1960). Patricia Meyer Spacks, "Logic and Language in 'Through the Looking Glass,'" *ETC.* 18 (1961): 91–100. Daniel F. Kirk, *Charles Dodgson, Semeiotician,* University of Florida Monographs: Humanities, 11 (Gainesville, Fla.: University of Florida Press, 1962). Gilles Deleuze, *Logique du sens* (Paris: Ed. de Minuit, 1969). Jacqueline Flescher, "The Language of Nonsense in *Alice*," *Yale French Studies,* no. 43 (1969), pp. 128–44. Warren Shibles, "A Philosophical Commentary on *Alice's Adventures in Wonderland*," *Wittgenstein, Language and Philosophy* (Dubuque, Iowa: W. C. Brown, 1969), pp. 14–45. Kathleen Blake, *Play, Games, and Sport: The Literary Works of Lewis Carroll* (Ithaca, N.Y.: Cornell University Press, 1974). Peter Heath, *The Philosopher's Alice* (New York: St. Martin's Press, 1974). Francis Huxley, *The Raven and the Writing Desk* (New York: Harper, 1976). Alwin L. Baum, "Carroll's *Alices:* The Semiotics of Paradox," *American Imago* 34 (1977): 86–108.

However, an article by Winfried Nöth, which I saw after this one was accepted for publication, does have a similar perspective: "Dialoganomalie und Nonsense in Alices Wunderland," *Dialoge: Beiträge zur Interaktions- und Diskursanalyse,* ed. Wilfried Heindrichs and G. C. Rump (Hildesheim: Gerstenberg, 1979), pp. 134–60.

4. "Rules and Regulations" is the title of a poem that Carroll wrote when he was thirteen. It includes the lines, "By permutation / In conversation / And deep reflection / You'll avoid dejection." Lewis Carroll, *Useful and Instructive Poetry,* ed. Derek Hudson (1954; reprint ed., n.p.: Folcroft, 1971), p. 38.

Charles W. Morris, a disciple of the pragmatist philosopher C. S. Peirce, coined the term "pragmatics" in 1938. Morris defined pragmatics as the study of "the relation of signs to interpreters"—a study different from the other two branches of "semiotic," that is, "semantics" and "syntactics." Charles W. Morris, *Foundations of the Theory of Signs,* International Encyclopedia of Unified Science, 1:2 (Chicago: University of Chicago Press, 1938), pp. 6–7. A few linguists would restrict the term to the study of indexical reference (deixis), but speech-act theory and related concerns are usually included.

Compact histories of the concept are provided by Ruth M. Kempson, *Presupposition and the Delimitation of Semantics,* Cambridge Studies in Linguistics, 15 (Cambridge: Cambridge University Press, 1975), pp. 137–38; and John Lyons, *Semantics* (Cambridge: Cambridge University Press, 1977), 1: 114–19. For lists of relevant books and articles see Gerald Gazdar, G. K. Pullum, and Ewan Klein, "A Bibliography of Pragmatics," *Pragmatics Microfiche* 2, no. 2 (August 1977); and the references in Gerald Gazdar's *Pragmatics: Implicature, Presupposition, and Logical Form* (New York: Academic Press, 1979).

5. I begin to discuss this topic in "How to Play Games with Words: Speech-Act Jokes," *Journal of Literary Semantics* 9 (1980): 20–29.

6. J. L. Austin, *How to Do Things with Words,* ed. J. O. Urmson (1962; reprint ed., New York: Oxford University Press, 1965). John R. Searle, *Speech Acts: An Essay in the Philosophy of Language* (Cambridge: Cambridge University Press, 1969).

7. Austin, *Words,* pp. 18, 34.

8. Austin, *Words,* p. 34.

9. Carroll, *Nursery "Alice,"* p. 16.

10. Strictly speaking, offering is commissive in force as well as directive; that is, to offer something to someone is to commit oneself to do something (i.e., to supply that thing), as well as to direct him to do something (i.e., to take that thing). A precondition on the successful performance of a commissive speech act is that the speaker think that he is able to do whatever it is that he commits himself to do. Evidently the March Hare's

offer to Alice fails in this respect also. I discuss the structure of offers and other commissive-directives in "The Classification of Cooperative Illocutionary Acts," *Language in Society* 8 (1979): 1–14.

11. H. P. Grice, "Logic and Conversation," *Speech Acts,* Syntax and Semantics, 3, ed. Peter Cole and J. L. Morgan (New York: Academic Press, 1975), pp. 41–58. Most of the phrases quoted in the next several paragraphs are from this paper, which has been excerpted from the William James Lectures that Grice gave at Harvard University in 1967–68.

12. A "regulative rule" prescribes a certain kind of behavior but is not definitive of or essential to that behavior. By contrast a "constitutive rule" actually defines (or helps to define) a certain kind of behavior. Searle, *Speech Acts,* pp. 33–42.

13. Representative studies by Sacks and his associates have been collected in *Studies in the Organization of Conversational Interaction,* ed. Jim Schenkein (New York: Academic Press, 1978), which includes a detailed bibliography.

14. Harvey Sacks, Emmanuel A. Schegloff, and Gail Jefferson, "A Simplest Systematics for the Organization of Turn Taking for Conversation," in *Studies,* ed. Schenkein, pp. 12–13.

15. Relevant essays by Robin Lakoff include "Language in Context," *Language* 48 (1972): 907–27; "The Logic of Politeness; or, Minding Your p's and q's," *Papers from the Ninth Regional Meeting, Chicago Linguistic Society* (Chicago: Chicago Linguistic Society, 1973), pp. 292–305; *Language and Woman's Place* (New York: Harper, 1975); and "What You Can Do with Words: Politeness, Pragmatics, and Performatives," *Proceedings of the Texas Conference on Performatives, Presuppositions, and Implicatures* (Arlington, Va.: Center for Applied Linguistics, 1977), pp. 79–105.

Penelope Brown and Stephen Levinson, "Universals in Language Usage: Politeness Phenomena," *Questions and Politeness: Strategies in Social Interaction,* ed. E. N. Goody, Cambridge Papers in Social Anthropology, 8 (Cambridge: Cambridge University Press, 1978), pp. 56–324.

16. Erving Goffman, "On Face-Work: An Analysis of Ritual Elements in Social Interaction," *Interaction Ritual: Essays on Face-to-Face Behavior* (Garden City, N.Y.: Doubleday-Anchor, 1967), p. 5.

17. Searle, *Speech Acts,* p. 66. See Robert L. Brown, Jr., "The Pragmatics of Verbal Irony," *Language Use and the Uses of Language,* ed. Roger W. Shuy and Anna Shnukal (Washington, D.C.: Georgetown University Press, 1980), pp. 111–27.

18. John R. Searle, "Indirect Speech Acts," *Speech Acts,* ed. Cole and Morgan, pp. 71–72.

19. So J. Vahlen (erroneously?) glossed Aristotle; see Gerald F. Else, *Aristotle's Poetics: The Argument* (Cambridge, Mass.: Harvard University Press, 1967), p. 344.

20. Stanley E. Fish, "How to Do Things with Austin and Searle: Speech Act Theory and Literary Criticism," *MLN* 91 (1976): 983–1025.